GAMING

Cruising the Casinos with
Syndicated Gambling Columnist
John Grochowski

RUNNING COUNT PRESS
P. O. Box 1488
Elmhurst, Illinois 60126
708-279-8309

ISBN 0-9653454-0-8

Printed in the U.S.A.

10 9 8 7 6 5 4 3 2 1

FOREWORD
By Anthony Curtis

In April, 1991, something strange happened in Iowa: People began gambling on riverboats. Legally! The launching of Iowa's riverboat casinos was a monumental event in the evolution of the U.S. gambling industry, since it marked the true beginning of gambling's emergence from its decades-long confinement to Las Vegas and Atlantic City. Indeed, it wasn't long before the same strange thing happened in Illinois—gambling boats set sail on the Mississippi in September that same year.

To no one's surprise, gambling was a hit in the Land of Lincoln. People flocked to the boats, their collective endorsement evident in the tally of boarding admissions and buy-ins. This indisputable demonstration of public approval ultimately led to the strangest occurrence of all. In 1994, the *Chicago Sun-Times,* one of the nation's largest newspapers, initiated a column about gambling. Not the political or business side of the industry, but a column designed to educate and inform gamblers, with a focus on the games themselves. There was no other newspaper column like it in the entire country—and that included the two Las Vegas dailies. Innovative and groundbreaking, yes. But did the *Sun-Times* have a writer with the firepower to pull it off?

One of the features of my Las Vegas Advisor newsletter is the monthly monitoring of "Gambling in the Media," in which we handicap the efforts of mainstream writers who dare to wade into the treacherous waters of gambling analysis. I got wind of the *Sun-Times* column just days after its inauguration, and while my colleagues at LVA and I rooted for the success of this undertaking, we couldn't help but be skeptical. Mostly, we wondered about the upstart writer (gambling-wise), whom we would surely have to take to task.

John Grochowski?

Never heard of him.

I remember hunkering down with that first column, a particularly well-sharpened red pencil at the ready.

Big surprise! The numbers were right. The grasp was solid. The column was good. It was the same with subsequent columns. John's advice was consistently accurate, honest, and devoid of the needless (and irresponsible) hype that is so common in this business.

I'm now a fan and regular reader of John's "Gaming" and "Casinos" columns in the *Sun-Times*. I enjoy them, but more importantly, I trust them. Nearly two years' worth of those columns are compiled in this book, and they contain information that can improve your prospects in the casinos. As you read this collection, I think you'll be entertained. I know you'll be educated.

Anthony Curtis publishes the monthly Las Vegas Advisor newsletter, is the author of Bargain City *and has published many other books on gambling.*

FOREWORD
By Lenny Frome

When it comes to gambling, truth is indeed stranger than fiction. Would anyone have believed that the first collection of "how-to" newspaper gambling articles would be published by a gambling columnist from Chicago, where gambling is in its infancy?

Why not Las Vegas, the Mecca of Gambling with 65 years of gambling history, or Philadelphia, with 18 years of casinos in its backyard, or Denver or Minneapolis? Even Los Angeles, fully aware that 35 percent of visitors to Las Vegas are Californians, would have seemed the right place to spawn such a breakthrough. How did this 100-1 shot manage to work out?

The answer is simple: The newspapers in these cities have rarely printed anything designed to help the casino players. A collection of all their articles would be a small pamphlet, at best. Of course, they would publish the pamphlet, useless as it might be, if the casinos would advertise heavily in it.

Hats off to the Chicago *Sun-Times* and especially to John Grochowski, whose foresight in bringing intelligence to his readers puts him a class above his colleagues in the newspaper business. He tells his readers what they need to know to be at ease in the casino, while letting them know that there are plenty of expert writers offering products such as books, PC software and videocassettes, and who are willing to answer questions to help them win more often. For this we of the community of gambling writers have John and the *Sun-Times* to thank.

Yet, as I watch the players everywhere hacking away at games that they know little or nothing about, whether it be the old standbys like video poker, craps or blackjack, or the newcomers like Caribbean Stud or Let It Ride, I can't help but feel we could use a dozen more forward-looking editors to make the public aware of how to survive better in casinos.

I sincerely hope that what the *Sun-Times* and John have accomplished serves to fuel a much broader effort to bring casino gambling out of the closet in the features departments so that soon Americans can all read a "Casino Parade" supplement in our Sunday newspapers.

The first step has been taken. And Chicagoans are better off for it. Who's next?

Lenny Frome, nationally known as a video poker expert, is author of Video Poker: America's National Game of Chance *along with many other books and booklets on video poker, Caribbean Stud and Let It Ride.*

INTRODUCTION

Most newspaper coverage of casino gambling is geared toward covering the politics and finances of the industry. The focus is on whether casinos will gain state approval, what restrictions will be placed on the industry, how much money the casinos are making and how much tax revenue is being generated.

Lost in the shuffle is that casino gambling is an entertainment industry. Millions of people play in casinos; combined attendance at the four Chicago area riverboat casino operations alone is more than 30,000 a day. And little is done to help these people get more for their casino entertainment dollar. A typical newspaper will tell its readers which theatrical plays, movies or television shows are better than others, but won't explain which casino offers a better set of blackjack rules, or how to get the most for your money on the slot machines, or which bets should be avoided at all costs.

That started to change in the Chicago *Sun-Times* in late 1993. Given the growth of the Illinois casino industry, reporters and editors were asked to suggest ways in which we could get consumer-oriented gambling information in the paper.

I was one of the *Sun-Times* employees who gave suggestions, and the result was that I was asked to write a weekly column. "Gaming" apparently struck a chord with readers. In the first two years of publication, I received more than 1,000 letters and faxes, and countless phone calls. Many are requests for back columns and reprints, requests that I find myself increasingly unable to fulfill as the number of columns mounts.

Recognizing that riverboat gambling was drawing customers who had never played in the traditional casino markets of Nevada and Atlantic City, I've tried to explain the basics for beginners while still keeping the column interesting for more experienced players. I've let the readers be my guide. You'll find the earliest columns are the most basic; sophisticated gambling questions by readers have taken me down paths I'd never imagined when I started writing this column.

Since its debut on February 18, 1994, "Gaming" has run every Friday in the *Sun-Times* WeekendPlus section. In October, 1994, the column went into syndication through the Chicago *Sun-Times* Features Syndicate, and now appears in several newspapers in the Midwest and South. A year later, in October, 1995, the column expanded to twice a week. It now also appears as "Casinos" in the Showcase section on Sundays.

And while the column's original mission was to provide information about playing on Chicago area riverboat casinos, most of "Gaming" and "Casinos" is applicable to any casino market. A special effort is taken to make at least one column each week suitable for syndication customers outside Chicago.

This book collects most of the columns published in the first year and a half "Gaming" appeared. Some were specific enough to their time that they have not been collected here—analyses of games whose conditions have changed drastically, details that have changed of train and bus fares to casino locations.

At the end of some columns in this book, you'll find author's notes to make necessary updates if conditions have changed. Where there was the odd error in the original column that I corrected weeks later, I changed the original column and dropped the correction for this book. An exception comes in the case of one early column; more information and further thought convinced me one of my answers to a letter was wrong. There, I judged the original letter and answer an essential part of the column, and added an explanatory author's note afterward.

In Chapters 1 through 65, you'll find columns that appeared in the Chicago *Sun-Times* from February, 1994, through July, 1995. Chapters 66 and 67 could be viewed almost as tryouts. They originally appeared in the *Sun-Times* Travel section—one already had been published, and the other was awaiting publication as "Gaming" was under discussion. They are pieces I asked the decision-makers to read when they were discussing whether to have me write "Gaming."

Special thanks go to *Sun-Times* employees, past and present, Tim Bannon, P.J. Bednarski, Kaarin Tisue, Avis Weathersbee, Jeff Johnson, Andrea Hanis, John Barron and Jack Schnedler; and to many people in and around the casino industry, including Anthony Curtis, Deke Castleman, Lenny Frome, Lorraine Nelson, Jim Murphy, Mary Phalen, Alissa Johnson, Kathy Posner and Howell Malham. Their help and encouragement has made "Gaming" a pleasure to write.

John Grochowski
May, 1996

TABLE OF CONTENTS

❧ 1 ❧
Lesson Number One:
The House Advantage

From every blackjack pit to every bank of slot machines, every craps table to every roulette wheel, there's one sure thing.

The casino expects to win.

An edge is built into every game that makes it inevitable: In the long run, the house will wind up with most of the money.

There are winners, of course. The house edge is narrow enough that in the short term anything can happen. Casinos need winners to spread the word.

The first step, though, to give yourself a chance to hold onto most of your money and sometimes even come out ahead, is to understand how the house gives itself the advantage. Here's where that edge comes from in some of the most commonly played games:

Blackjack: The lone house advantage is that the player gets the first chance to bust—draw cards totaling more than 21. A player who busts loses the bet, regardless of whether the dealer busts.

That means every player, from the novice to the card-counting expert, loses more hands than he or she wins.

The house gives back some of the edge by paying 3-2 on a blackjack— a two-card 21—and allowing the player to split pairs (play two hands) and double down (double the bet while taking a single card after the initial two).

Roulette: It's the zero and double zero on the American wheel that send bettors reeling. There are 36 other numbers, and a bet on a single number pays 35-1. But with zero and double zero, there are 38 numbers, making true odds 37-1. The zeroes are neither red nor black, odd nor even. If they come up, even-money bets go for naught. If you bet on black, it pays even money, but there are 20 losing spaces and only 18 winners.

Craps: Lucky seven is the culprit on the pass-line bet, most common at the table. Of 36 possible combinations on two dice, six total seven. That's good news on the first roll—a winner seven is the most likely number to hit. And with two ways to make 11 tossed in, there are eight first-roll winners and only four losers—the 2, 3 (two combinations) or 12, called craps. But if the roll is a 4 through 10, the shooter must repeat that number before another 7 comes up for the pass bet to win. Now 7, the most likely roll, works against the bettor. It all adds up to a 1.41 percent house edge.

Mini-baccarat: No decisions for the player to make here. The dealer gives additional cards to banker or player according to a set formula that ensures the banker will win more hands, good for a 1.24 percent edge. The house makes up for banker's natural edge by charging a 5 percent commission on winning banker bets.

Slot machines: A microprocessor with a random number generator determines when the jackpots hit. Each machine is programmed to pay out a certain percentage, though the big one could hit twice in a row, or not at all in billions of trials.

Video poker: Each hand is dealt from a randomly shuffled 52-card electronic deck. Average payout is determined by the pay table printed on the glass of each machine. Most commonly adjusted are payouts for full houses and flushes. In the full-pay version of Jacks or Better that returns 9-for-1 on a full house and 6-for-1 on a flush (a 9-6 machine, in video poker parlance), expert players buck a house edge of only one-half of 1 percent. If the casino decreases paybacks to 8-for-1 on a full house and 5-for-1 on a flush (an 8-5 machine), the house edge against experts increases to 2.7 percent. Most players give back a couple more percent with mistakes.

2

A Hands-Off Approach
To Blackjack Etiquette

Andy LaChapelle remembers what he was taught to do in the old days if a player picked up his cards at the blackjack table.

"You slap his hands," says LaChapelle, director of casino operations at Harrah's Joliet.

Of course, that's not how LaChapelle, with 16 years in the gaming industry, instructs his gaming hosts to deal with the situation.

Harrah's touts its smiling gaming hosts, rather than having traditional, intimidating pit bosses, floormen and dealers. With so many first-time casino-goers streaming to Illinois riverboats, the emphasis is on customers' comfort. The last thing the casino wants to do is scare 'em off.

"We tell our people in our school, 'We need you to be good enough to discern whether this is a rookie customer who doesn't know, or whether he does know,'" says LaChapelle.

"We tell both to please put the cards down, but to one we might say, 'Honey, you don't even have to touch those cards. I do all the work here,' and the other we might look directly in the eye and say, 'Sir, do you understand what I'm saying?'"

All players' cards are dealt face up in the Illinois riverboats' multiple-deck games, and there's no need to touch them. Despite best efforts by dealers to be friendly and helpful, some novices find little procedures like that intimidating, leading most first-timers to head straight for the slot machines. But the procedures are really very simple, and a little knowledge can ease the tension.

So, for beginners, here's what to expect at the blackjack table:

Betting limits: A sign at each table tells the minimum and maximum bets accepted. In the Chicago area, $5 is the least you can bet.

Buying chips: Sit down at one of the seven betting spots and put money on the table in front of you. If the dealer is in the middle of a hand, he or she will finish before making change. Say, "Change please," or "Chips please," and the dealer will take the money and give you an equivalent amount of chips.

Making a bet: Directly in front of you will be a betting square. Place a chip or chips in the square. If betting more than one chip, stack them on top of each other, in denomination order, with the smallest denomination on top.

The deal: Each player receives two cards dealt face up, while the dealer receives one face up and one face down.

Playing the hand: Starting at "first base," the betting position all the way to the players' right, players decide in turn whether to hit—draw a card—or stand. Hitting or standing decisions are made with hand signals—a verbal request to hit or stand will give away your novice status. A flattened palm over the table signifies stand; an index finger pointed at the cards or a hand motion toward you signifies a hit. You can take as many cards as you like as long as your total is less than 21.

If you bust—draw cards totaling more than 21—the dealer will take away your cards and your bet. After all players either stand or bust, the dealer plays out his hand, standing on all totals of 17 or more, hitting 16 or less. After the dealer has either busted or reached a total of 17 or better, he pays the players who have bettered his total and collects the bets from those who have not.

Easy, huh? There are other options—splitting pairs, doubling down, insurance—but that's a subject for another time.

❧ 3 ❧
Reader Asks: How Honest
Are One-Armed Bandits?

Our first shuffle through the Gaming mailbag:

DEAR JOHN: *My four sisters and myself have lost thousands of dollars on slot machines. We honestly believed and hoped that we could win sometimes, and never have. Now we want to know the truth.*

What control over the slot machines does the management or owners have? What are the odds of anyone winning the $1,000, $5,000 or jackpot amounts? Are the machines rigged? Are the riverboat casino slot machines regulated by the government as far as their payouts go?

– Kathleen Springer, Chicago

Answer: Relax, the games are honest. It sounds like your expectations and money management strategy might need some fine-tuning, though.

Payouts on electronic gaming devices—that includes video poker, video blackjack and video keno as well as reel slots—are regulated by the Illinois Gaming Board. No machine may pay back less than 80 percent of money played, and no machine may pay back more than 100 percent.

Within those limits, manufacturers program payback percentages to casinos' specifications. The Gaming Board reveals actual payouts each month. The Empress typically comes in at about 93.5 percent, with Harrah's and the Hollywood boats just under 93 percent.

The big jackpots are factored into those percentages. It takes thousands, even tens of thousands, of pulls to support a $1,000 jackpot depending on the frequency of smaller payouts; tens of thousands to support a $5,000 jackpot, and perhaps millions to support one of the big progressive payoffs.

Average payback percentages are based on payouts over 100,000 to 300,000 handle pulls. There is plenty of room for runs of good and bad luck in so many plays.

"You can pull 100 times and not get anything back, or you can pull five times and get $300," says Roger Shields of the Gaming Board.

The reason is the random number generator built into the computer chip that drives the machine. Each possible combination of reels is assigned a number or numbers. Numbers are generated continuously. Whichever number is up when you pull the handle determines where the reels will stop.

If a jackpot combination is assigned one number out of 10,000, the jackpot will show up, on the average, one of 10,000 pulls. However, because the numbers are random, that combination could come up twice in a row. But the machine is never "due." If you've pulled the handle 9,999 times, there still is only a one-in-10,000 chance of that jackpot showing up on the next pull.

Gaming Board safeguards are extensive.

"The casino can't just open the door on a machine, turn a set screw and change the percentage," says Shields.

"When he opens the door, a slot technician can access the hopper, the coin box, the reels, but he can't get into the internal heart of the machine. It's locked separately and sealed with evidence tape."

The computer chip inside also is sealed with evidence tape.

You can be confident the results are random, but it sounds as though your problem might be giving back all the smaller returns while chasing big jackpots. That's not unusual among slot players. Just be aware that if you put all the returns back into the machines, you risk ending up with nothing.

DEAR JOHN: *Regarding craps, are there double the odds, or more, on casino riverboats? In blackjack, do the rules for dealer hits on soft 17 vary from casino to casino? Do the riverboats offer single-deck blackjack, or only multiple deck? And concerning blackjack strategy, if the dealer is showing a 6 and I have a two-card 16, should I hit? What if I have a three-card 16?*

— Tom Bromgard, Chicago

Answer: You'll be happy to know that the Chicago area boats—the Empress, Harrah's and Hollywood—all offer double odds in craps.

Blackjack games are all multiple deck—six decks on Harrah's and the Empress, eight at Hollywood—with players' cards dealt face up. Dealers stand on all 17s, including soft 17 (ace-6 is a two-card soft 17).

As for hitting 16 against a 6—don't. It doesn't matter if your 16 is two, three or more cards, give the dealer the chance to bust. Basic strategy calls for the player to hit all 16s if the dealer shows a 7 or better, but stand on hard 16 against 2 through 6.

❧ 4 ❧
Managing Your Money
At the Slot Machines

A quick quiz:

You've boarded one of the riverboat casinos with a $100 bankroll. Within the first five minutes you've hit a $200 jackpot on a quarter slot machine.

Do you:

A. Shout "Hooray!" and return to shore before the boat leaves the dock.

B. Pocket the $200 and keep playing your original stake.

C. Pocket your original $100 but play more aggressively, using the jackpot.

D. Move to $1 slot machines because now you're playing with "their money."

If you've bought a cruise ticket, you're probably planning on a couple hours worth of casino entertainment and aren't likely to choose A, even though it assures a big payday. Players who choose B are certain to leave the boat with a profit, and players who choose C will leave no worse than even.

So A, B and C can all be regarded as financially sound, though A and B are wiser than C.

But players who choose D are the ones who never leave the casino with a profit. Often they leave their entire bankroll in the machines.

All that, because they've not learned a money management basic:

It's not "their money." And you don't have to give it back.

A little discipline and some money management skills can help you leave the casino with more of *your* money, whether you hit a big jackpot or not.

Money management starts at home, with a decision on how much money to bring to the casino. (*Never* gamble with money you can't afford to lose.)

Don't overbet your bankroll. If you're bringing $100 for a cruise, you can't afford to play the $1 slot machines. In a cold streak, they can eat that up in five minutes flat. Stick to quarters.

Most important, discipline yourself to walk away when you're losing. The more you play, the more the house percentage has a chance to work against you.

One technique I like is to divide the day's stake into session bankrolls, figuring five half-hour sessions in a two-and-a-half hour cruise.

In the case of our $100 low-roller, that would leave $20, or two rolls of quarter tokens, for each 30 minutes.

First buy $20 of change. No matter how your luck runs, don't touch the remaining $80 during that half hour. Run the coins through a machine once. If the returns give you more than $20, put the profit in your pocket, and replay only the original stake.

If the payback is less than $20, then play whatever's left. If, for example, your return the first time through is $15, play that. Then if the payback is more than $15 on the second time around, pocket the profit and replay only the $15. If the payback is less than $15, play the remainder.

Any time your payback is less money than you play, consider changing machines to play what's left. There's no way to tell when a machine is going to pay off, but moving every so often at least gives you a chance to take a deep breath and clear your head.

When the half hour expires, pocket whatever is left of that session stake and buy a fresh $20.

However, if at any time you play the session stake down to zero, you're finished for the rest of that 30 minutes. Explore the ship's other decks. Watch the roulette wheel. Go up top and get a breath of fresh air. Then get ready to play your next session bankroll in the following half hour.

If you happen to hit a big jackpot, put at least half of it away. You can increase your stake, but be sure to walk away a winner.

Above all, avoid the common slot player's trap of replaying every return until there's nothing left. Putting portions of the returns away as you go along won't guarantee wins, but it can cut the losses.

❧ 5 ❧

Fast-Rolling Craps Can
Be Baffling to Newcomer

It's fast. It's exciting. And it offers some of the best odds in the house. But to a newcomer, craps also can be baffling. Intimidating.

"It's the speed," says Ed Devlin, a shift manager for the Hollywood Casino in Aurora. "In blackjack, you control your own hand, but in craps, every roll comes quickly."

It's also the sheer number of bets available. That can be mind-boggling to a beginning dealer, let alone a beginning player.

Says Andy LaChapelle, director of casino operations at Harrah's Joliet: "In the 10th week of craps school—and I'd rather go to jail than to go through craps school—these kids asked, 'Would you extend the school two more weeks? We want to be ready for you.'

"It's an incredibly complex game to learn how to deal. There are 30 or 40 ways to bet at one time, and the gaming host has to know all of them."

But the novice player doesn't need to know every bet on the table. And the game can be simple to pick up as you go along if you pick an uncrowded table at a less busy time and position yourself close to a dealer.

"The perfect opportunity to learn is to come midweek in the daytime, find a slow craps game and snuggle right up to the dealer's base and tell 'em you've never been here before and would like to learn to play," says LaChapelle. "You'll get a blinding smile, because these kids are busting at the gate to show what they know."

For those contemplating trying craps for the first time, here's what to expect in the way of personnel and procedures. Next week, we'll go over available bets and odds.

Table personnel: At the center of one side of the table is the boxman, who supervises the game and takes cash collected by the dealers and deposits it in a drop box. Directly opposite him is the stickman, who uses a stick to push the dice to the shooter. He controls the tempo of the game. On the sides are two dealers, who take bets, pay off winners and collect losing bets.

Layout: At the center of the table between the boxman and stickman are boxes for proposition bets—one-roll bets on 7, 11, 2, 3, 12 or any craps (2, 3 or 12)—and hard-way bets—betting that the 6, for example, will show up as two 3s before either a 7 or any other 6 is rolled. Hard-way bets also are available on 4, 8 and 10. On either side is the pass line—a bar that extends all around the table for players betting with the shooter. There is a smaller don't pass bar for players betting against the shooter. A large area in the center marked "come" and a corresponding "don't come" area are for bets similar to pass/don't pass, at different points in the game.

Across the layout on the side by the boxman are boxes with the numbers 4, 5, 6, 8, 9 and 10, for "place" or "buy" bets that the number chosen will be rolled before a 7.

Buying chips: Place money on the layout and ask a dealer for change. The dealer will call out, "Change only," the boxman will count out the money and supervise as the dealer gives you an equivalent amount of chips. "A very important fact is that the dealer cannot take money out of your hand," says Devlin. "If you reach across the table and try to hand the dealer money, the dealer will say, 'Put the money on the layout.'"

Placing a bet: You can make your own pass line bets by placing chips in the pass area directly in front of you. For proposition bets, place chips on the table in front of you and ask the dealer for the bet. The dealer will move the chips to the appropriate place on the layout.

❧ 6 ❧

Basics at the Craps Table:
The Pass-Line Wager

Want an easy bet on the craps table?

Many newcomers start with a bet on the field. It's a one-roll bet, seven numbers win (2, 3, 4, 9, 10, 11 and 12) and two of them (2 and 12) pay off at 2-1.

Problem is, it's a bet that gives the casino a 5.5 percent advantage. And in this game, you can do much better.

Do you want a good bet?

A pass-line wager, backed with the double odds allowed by Harrah's, the Hollywood and the Empress, cuts the house edge to six-tenths of 1 percent.

This bet confuses many novices, partly because it frequently takes several rolls to determine an outcome.

The betting sequence starts with the come-out roll. If the shooter is coming out, a plastic disk, black side up with the word "Off" in white, will be placed on a corner of the layout, usually in a box marked "Don't Come." If the disk has been flipped over to its white side, labeled "On" and placed in a numbered box, that number is the current point and the roll is not a come-out.

To make a pass bet, place a chip or chips in the area in front of you marked "Pass Line." The bet pays even money; that is, if you bet $5 and win, you'll receive another $5.

If the shooter rolls a 7 or 11, you win. If he rolls a 2, 3, or 12, that's craps and you lose. If he rolls any other number, it becomes the point.

Now the shooter must roll the same number again before he rolls a 7. If the 7 comes first, pass bets lose.

The house edge on this bet is 1.41 percent, but here's the good part. After a point is established, you may place twice your original bet behind it as your double odds wager. This bet, unlike any other in the house, is paid off at true odds, reducing the house advantage in the pass/odds combination to 0.6 percent.

An example: You bet a $5 chip on the pass line. A 6 turns up on the come-out roll. That becomes the point. Now you put $10 in chips directly behind your original bet. True odds against a 6 coming up before a 7 are 6-5, because there are six ways to roll a 7 with two dice and only five ways to roll 6.

So if that 6 comes up, you'll receive $5 to pay off your pass bet and $12 for your $10 odds bet.

Odds bets pay 6-5 on a 6 or 8, 3-2 on 5 or 9 and 2-1 on 4 or 10.

There's also an area of the layout marked "Don't Pass." Here, you win if a 2 or 3 turn up on the come-out roll or, if a point is established, a 7 is rolled before the point number comes up again.

The house keeps its 1.4 percent edge here by "barring" the 12. The house neither pays nor takes the bet if a 12 is rolled in the come-out, even though 12 is a loser for the pass bettor.

The don't bettor also may "lay" odds, giving the house the same odds the house gives a pass bettor on his odds wager.

Here are some other bets available. Don't get bogged down in the numbers; you can forget most of these wagers. Unless you need to have a lot of action on each roll, stick to pass/don't pass, come/don't come and, perhaps, place bets on the 6 and 8:

Come/Don't Come: The same as pass/don't pass, except the wager is not made on the come-out roll. You may back come bets with odds, leaving the house a 0.6 percent edge.

For example, if the point is established as 5 on the come-out, you now may place a come bet. If the next number rolled is 9, that is the point for your come bet. If you wish, you may make another come bet on the next roll. However, just as on a pass bet, if a 7 shows up before that 9, you lose.

Place/Buy bets: Instead of waiting for a number to show up as a point for a pass or come bet, you may "place" the number. Place bets on the 4 or 10 are paid are 9-5, for a house edge of 6.67 percent, the 5 and 9 are paid at 7-5 (4 percent edge) and the 6 and 8 at 7-6 (1.52 percent). You also may "buy" the numbers by giving the house a 5 percent commission. In exchange, the casino pays buy bets at true odds. Since the house edge is less than 5 percent on the 5, 6, 8 and 9, it doesn't pay to buy these numbers. Buying the 4 or 10 can reduce the edge to 4.76 percent.

Hardways: There are four hardway numbers—4, 6, 8 and 10. The number is rolled the hard way when both dice show the same number—that is, a hard 6 is two 3s. On a hardway wager, the number chosen must come up hard before a 7 or before the number shows up any other way. House edge is 11.1 percent on the 4 or 10, 9.09 percent on the 6 or 8.

Proposition bets: These are one-roll bets shown on the center of the layout—any 7, any craps, 2, 12, 3 and 11 among them. They all carry huge house edges, from 11.1 percent on any craps to 16.67 percent on any 7. Avoid them.

So do you want to cut the house edge to the minimum?

Make a pass-line bet, to be backed with full double odds if a point is established. Follow with come bets until you have three numbers working, all backed with double odds.

You'll be working against the one of the lowest edges in the casino.

❧ 7 ❧
Debunking the Flawed
Martingale System

A shuffle through the Gaming mailbag:

DEAR JOHN: *Please comment on the enclosed blackjack strategy related to me by a friend. He tried it just last week and won $200 before leaving the table. Also, what are the odds of losing eight hands in a row and thus tapping out the bank?*

Bet $5. If you lose, double it to $10; if you lose, double it to $20 and so on. If you win, go back to your initial bet of $5. You will make money if you have a large enough bank to withstand a series of losing hands. A seriously unlucky streak of losing seven hands in a row would require a bankroll of $1,275 to make the eighth bet of $640. Never double down. Never split pairs. Never take insurance.

— Arthur Rummler, Evanston

Answer: This is an old system, called the Martingale. Nearly every gambling text that includes a discussion of betting systems includes a warning never to use this one. It's a crazy system, a system for financial disaster.

The Martingale will allow you to win more often than you lose, but a single loss will wipe out the profits of hundreds of wins.

Each hand you win will give an overall profit of $5 for the sequence. For example, if you've lost at $5, $10 and $20, a win at $40 would wipe out the $35 in losses and give you a $5 profit.

But do you really want to have a $640 bet on the line in hope of a $5 profit? That's more than my stomach could handle.

In your eight-step system, an average player will lose about once per 140 sequences, based on the house winning 54 percent of decisions. (A perfect basic strategy player can bring that down to less than 53 percent, leading to one loss per 170 sequences.)

The 139 sequences an average player wins will bring $695, plus 3-2 payoffs on approximately 15 blackjacks, almost all at the small bet levels that occur most frequently.

The one losing sequence will cost $1,275.

If the casinos were in any danger of losing to this system, a simple response would take care of it: Lower the betting maximums. In fact, aboard the Empress II in Joliet last week I found $500 maximums at $5 tables. That limits the Martingale to seven bets. The eighth bet of $640 would exceed the table maximum.

DEAR JOHN: *Why doesn't Illinois have live poker such as hold 'em or seven-card stud like they have in Iowa?*

– Jim Sauer, Des Plaines

Answer: Casinos can make more money using the space for slot machines or other table games. The house takes a percentage of each pot at live poker, but it has no control over the size of the pots or the speed of the game. That makes it the least profitable game for the casino. "If you have seven people playing, all taking their time over their cards, it could take 15 minutes to play a hand," said Ed Devlin, casino shift manager at the Hollywood in Aurora. "It's tough for us to offer any game we can't control the volume and speed of play."

DEAR JOHN: *If a friend and I go to the same craps table, he plays only the don't side and I bet with the dice. Why aren't we assured to be winners? Speaking of wrong (don't pass) bettors, I often see guys walk up to the table, put down $300, $400 or $500 bets, hang around for two or three rolls and walk away winners. Do these high-rollers know something that I don't know?*

– Alan Cole, Skokie

Answer: If a 12 comes up on the come-out, pass bets lose and don't pass bets push; that's the house edge on don't bets. On that 12, you'd lose and your friend would just keep his original bet. That's why this system loses in the long run.

As for those high-rolling don't bettors, the biggest thing they seem to know is to walk away with their winnings. Over the long haul, they face as big a house edge as the pass-line bettors.

DEAR JOHN: *There seems to be a double standard in the gambling industry in Illinois. At age 18 you can play the Illinois Lottery or go to the horse races, bet legally and no one cares. But riverboat gambling is a no-no if you are under 21. Seems to me the Gaming Board is nothing but a bunch of hypocrites.*

– Pat Knoth, Franklin Park

Answer: Your argument's not with the Gaming Board, it's with the state Legislature. Legal gambling ages were set by state law in the separate bills legalizing horse racing, the lottery and riverboat casinos. By the way, the Gaming Board has no control over horse racing, which is governed by the Illinois Racing Board, nor the lottery, governed by the Illinois Lottery Commission.

❀ 8 ❀

Betting on a New Career:
Casinos' Dealers Schools

To experienced dealers, it's automatic, done dozens if not hundreds of times a day:

Take a stack of chips—checks, as the casino people call them—divide them into smaller, even stacks to count them out, restack and push them to the player.

They could do it in their sleep.

But these aren't experienced dealers. It's school time at Harrah's Joliet, where security guards and food servers, player-tracking hosts and parking valets are learning to become gaming hosts.

And for Dominick Lofrano, a player-tracking host in his last week of blackjack school, his first tries at cutting checks still bring shudders.

"It looked so easy," Lofrano says, "but the first time I started I went..." and his voice trails off as he knocks chips all over the layout. "It's embarrassing, especially when you have to use two hands."

"It's even harder with small hands," laughs Karen Hanson, a food server at Andreotti's, Harrah's Italian restaurant.

Like the Empress in Joliet and the Hollywood boats in Aurora, Harrah's runs its own dealers school. On this day, with blackjack and roulette schools in session, all the trainees already are Harrah's employees, well-versed in the organization's "friendly attitude comes first" philosophy. Some are learning to deal their second or third game; most are trying to transfer from other departments.

Some of those transferring, though working for a casino operation, have never actually been in the casino.

"I worked in the pavilion, so this is a new world for me," says Hanson. "I did a banquet one time on the boat, but that's the only time I've been on board."

That's the way it goes at all three Chicago area operations. Openings are posted in-house first, and it's rare that dealers schools are opened to outside people.

At the Hollywood, says casino shift manager Ed Devlin, "If someone from the outside wanted to be a dealer at the Hollywood now, they probably couldn't get in.

"It's a good job, and we prefer to promote from within. Dealers make minimum wage of $4.25 per hour, and the toke (tip) rate averages $15 to $16 per hour."

Jim Murphy, marketing director of the Empress, suggests that anyone who wants to become a dealer should apply for a job "anywhere in the operation. After six months, they're eligible to transfer to a different job.

"Dealer is a low-turnover position. We lose some dealers to other boats and some to new operations in the South. The casino business can be very nomadic, but Midwestern people are not. We don't have the same turnover here, people hopping from casino to casino, that maybe you have in Atlantic City or Las Vegas."

Turnover can be a bit higher at Harrah's, with gaming hosts from Joliet moving to new Harrah's operations in Tunica and Vicksburg, Miss., with New Orleans and Shreveport, La., opening soon.

"We're only one step ahead," says casino manager Al Sikirdji. "We may reach the point where we have to go outside, with people going to Louisiana and Mississippi to work as supervisors."

To Tina Daliege, a blackjack dealer since October, hopes of becoming a supervisor are part of the reason she's in roulette school.

"This game is harder than blackjack. There's a lot more to watch, a lot more action," she says. "And if I want to work toward being a supervisor, it's to my advantage to add another game."

❧ 9 ❧

Are Blackjack Decks
Stacked Against Players?

A shuffle through the Gaming mailbag:

DEAR JOHN: *When the casino uses one or more decks in blackjack, do the odds for the house increase as more decks are used? Do video poker machines have a microprocessor that programs the number of times a straight flush and/or royal flush comes up? You mentioned that most players give the house a couple of percentage points because of mistakes. Are these errors due to playing too fast, or is it because the player doesn't know the odds in various hands?*

– Bruce, no address

Answer: The more decks used in blackjack, the bigger the house edge, provided other game conditions are the same. One reason is that blackjacks, which pay 3-2, occur slightly more frequently in a single-deck game than in multi-deckers. Let's say your first card is an Ace. In a single-deck game, 16 of the remaining 51 cards, or 31.4 percent, are 10-value cards that would complete a blackjack. In an eight-deck game, as you'll find at the Hollywood in Aurora and some Empress tables in Joliet, 128 of the remaining 415 cards, or 30.8 percent, have a value of 10 and would complete a blackjack.

As for video poker, the microprocessor has a random number generator, just like any other slot machine, that determines which card combinations come up.

According to Lenny Frome, whose *Video Poker: America's National Game of Chance* is the classic in its field, optimum play will result in a royal flush about once every 40,000 hands. The biggest mistake video poker players make is not playing the maximum number of coins, thereby giving up their chance for the big 4,000-coin payoff on a royal flush.

Other mistakes come on decisions about what cards to keep. For example, many players will keep a single Jack or better rather than a small pair, but keeping the pair is the better play. And never draw to an inside straight, unless it contains at least three high cards that could be paired for a Jacks or better payoff.

DEAR JOHN: *I would like to know if 25-cent video poker machines have a separate pay program for each coin. If this wasn't true, a person could play one coin most of the time, then switch to five coins if the machine wasn't paying well.*

– C. Jarmuth, Chicago

Answer: The machine doesn't "know" whether you're playing maximum coins, and it makes no adjustment to the cards you're dealt. That doesn't mean you'll get exactly the same cards no matter what you do. Hitting the "bet one" button, then the "deal" button takes a fraction of a second longer than hitting "maximum bet." That allows the random number generator to run a fraction of a second longer, meaning a different hand will be selected. Whether that hand is better or worse than if you'd gone the other way is pure chance.

DEAR JOHN: *I understand many of the casinos on the local riverboats offer very few gambling tables with a $5 minimum bet, and these tables usually have waiting lines. Could you advise me which boats have the most $5 minimum tables in blackjack or craps?*

– Gail Faber, Wheaton

Answer: This is mostly a matter of timing. On weekends, betting limits go up and you'll be lucky to find a spot at a $5 table. In daylight hours on weekdays, however, it's usually not much trouble. In the last few weeks I took midweek, daytime cruises on Harrah's Southern Star, Empress II and Hollywood's City of Lights I and had no trouble getting to $5 tables on any of them. On the lower level of Empress II, I even found $5 tables at which I was able to play head-to-head with the dealer.

DEAR JOHN: *In craps, assuming a point is established on the come-out roll, am I correct that statistically a don't player is at no advantage to lay odds because they are true? My friends say the casinos pay true odds when a pass bettor backs up his point, so a don't player should do the same because the house always has the advantage. I disagree.*

– No name

Answer: Statistically, you're exactly right. The danger point for a don't pass bettor is the come-out roll; there you have eight ways to lose (six ways to make 7, two to make 11) and only three ways to win (the 2 and two ways to make 3; 12 is a push). But once a point is established, the don't bettor is the favorite—odds are 6-5 in your favor on 6 or 8; 3-2 on 5 or 9, and 2-1 on 4 or 10.

So laying the odds after a point is established can be seen as watering down your mathematical edge, and my inclination is to skip the odds on a don't bet. Still, laying the odds is an even wager, and you'll not find many even wagers in the house.

AUTHOR'S NOTE: I've changed my position on this last answer since the original publication of this column on April 22, 1994. A don't bettor is, in fact, better off to reserve part of his intended don't pass wager in order to lay the odds if a point is established. The reason is that making a smaller don't pass wager reduces the bettor's exposure on the come-out roll, when there are eight ways to lose and only three ways to win. Laying the odds still isn't as good a bet as the don't wager that's working once a point has been established, but it's a much better bet than the don't wager on the come-out.

❧ 10 ❧
Be a Wheel Watcher:
How to Play Roulette

Compared with other table games, roulette proceeds at a stately, almost majestic pace.

Far from the 100 or more rolls an hour expected at a craps table or even the 60 hands an hour played at a busy blackjack table, the roulette wheel spins only 30 to 45 times each hour. The players need time to choose among the dozens of wagering possibilities, then the wheel is spun and a ball sent whirling in the opposite direction, until the ball finally settles into one of 38 numbered slots on the wheel.

The game is a favorite among Europeans, and even though the American wheel, with both a zero and double zero, offers less favorable odds than the European single-zero version, overseas visitors frequently crowd Las Vegas roulette tables.

Despite the array of wagers available, roulette is remarkably simple and relaxed. Still, the game has an etiquette all its own, with elements unlike those of any other table game. Here are some things you'll need to know when walking up to play roulette for the first time:

The wheel and layout: There are 38 numbered slots on the wheel, 1 through 36 as well as 0 and 00. Eighteen numbers are painted in black backgrounds, 18 in red. The backgrounds for 0 and 00 are green.

That all corresponds to a rectangular table layout with boxes for Nos. 1-36 arranged in 12 rows of three, and three columns of 12. The number in each box is surrounded by either a red or black background, the same color that corresponds to that number on the wheel.

Outside the numbered boxes, there are several other boxes for bets encompassing up to 18 numbers at a time. There is a box for each 12-number column, as well as red, black, even, odd, 1-18, 19-36, first 12, second 12 and third 12.

Table personnel: Usually, one dealer makes change, spins the wheel, keeps track of play, pays off winning bets and collects losing wagers. Sometimes a second dealer will be assigned to help at a busy wheel.

Buying chips: Just as at any other table, wait until after a hand has been finished, place your money on the layout—do not hand it to the dealer—and ask for chips.

There is a difference, though. At roulette, you will not be given regular casino chips. Instead, each player is given chips of a different color so the dealer can keep track of which bet belongs to which player. The player may designate what his chips will be worth.

At the $5 minimum-bet tables common in Illinois, the minimum chip value is $1 each, and that's what most players use. However, you may ask the dealer for $5 chips, or any other denomination above the minimum. He or she will place one of the chips of your color on a rail near the wheel and place a marker atop it to signify the denomination.

When you are ready to leave the game, ask the dealer to cash you out and place your remaining chips on the layout. The dealer will give you an equivalent amount of regular casino chips.

Because the same color can have different values at the same wheel over the course of a day, roulette chips have no value away from the wheel. The cashier's cage will not accept them. You must cash them in for regular casino chips before you leave the wheel.

☙ 11 ❧

An Inside-Outside Look
At Roulette Wagering

Beginning roulette players often are confused by the different rules for placing "inside" and "outside" bets.

Inside bets are those placed in the area where individual numbers are shown. At a table with a $5 minimum bet, a player may spread his $5 or more in chips worth at least $1 across several numbers or combinations of numbers.

But on the outside—where bets such as red/black or odd/even are shown—most casinos require a full $5 on any one bet. If you wish to bet on black, you must place at least a $5 wager in that rectangle. If you also wish to bet on odd, it will cost you another $5.

Here's an overview of available bets:

Outside bets: Three bets—red/black, odd/even, 1 through 18/19 through 36—pay even money. A bet on red, for example, would win if the ball lands on any of the 18 numbers shown on a red background on the layout and on the wheel.

Bets on the first 12, second 12 and third 12, and bets on any of the three columns of 12 numbers on the layout, pay 2-1.

Zero and 00, shown in green on the layout and the wheel, are neither odd nor even, neither red nor black. If either shows up, all outside bets lose.

Inside bets: Wagers on individual numbers, placed by putting a chip or chips fully inside the box for a number, including 0 and 00, pay 35-1. You also can bet inside numbers in several different combinations.

A chip straddling the line between two numbers is called a split bet. If either number hits, it pays 17-1.

A three-number bet, called a street, is made by placing a chip on the line separating the inside from the outside, indicating a row of three consecutive numbers, such as 1, 2 and 3. It pays 11-1.

Move the chip so that it straddles two rows of numbers as well as the inside/outside line, and you have a six-number double street, paying 5-1.

One of the most common bets is the corner, with a chip placed at the intersection of four numbers. If any of the four comes up, the bet pays 8-1.

The least popular wager at the table is the five-number combination of 0, 00, 1, 2 and 3, placed much like a double street, with the chip straddling the line between 0-00 and the 1-2-3 row. It pays 5-1.

There's a good reason the lone five-number combination is rarely placed. The house edge on the bet is 7.37 percent.

On every other bet on an American wheel, the house edge is 5.26 percent.

Let's say you you bet the same single number each spin. Because there are 38 numbers including 0 and 00, on the average you'll win one of every 38 spins. On that one, you'll be paid 35 chips and you'll keep the one you bet. The house keeps two of 38—or 5.26 percent.

The house edge is reduced to 2.7 percent on a European wheel with just one 0. You'll not find any of these in Illinois, and it takes some work to find one in Las Vegas or Atlantic City. European casinos also feature the "en prison" rule—if the ball lands on 0, even-money bets do not lose, but must stay on the table for the next spin. If the 0 comes up a second consecutive time, then the bet loses. This lowers the house edge on even-money bets to 1.4 percent—one of the better bets in the house.

❧ 12 ❧

Betting Strategies Differ
In Tournament Blackjack

A shuffle through the Gaming mailbag:

DEAR JOHN: *During our twice-a-year Wisconsin fishing trips, my two brothers and I take a day and drive just across the border to the Grand Casino at Hinckley, Minn. I head straight for the nickel poker machines, but I make an exception by playing in a weekly blackjack tournament the casino conducts.*

Everyone receives $500 worth of chips (no real cash value) and plays 30 hands in a preliminary round at tables with seven players. The player who wins the most at each table advances.

My question has to do with how to bet. I have been betting $15 per hand for 25 hands and then spreading any winnings over the last five hands. So far, the best I've done is to finish with second-best winnings.

Is there a specific betting strategy that would give one the best possibility of finishing with a winning total?

– Dan McGuire, Bensenville

Answer: It sounds like you're doing just fine. Anthony Curtis, publisher of the monthly Las Vegas Advisor newsletter, says, "He's already doing the most important thing, and that's betting all his money at some time during the round.

"I liken it to a gunfight and the chips are the bullets he has to shoot. If you don't shoot sometime, you're not going to win. As an ancillary benefit, by keeping his bets low early, he's giving himself a chance to win without having to fire if some other players lose big bets.

"It's about as good a strategy as he can have, for now. That won't always be true. As the players get better (in newer gambling markets) he'll have to employ different strategies, finding opportunities to bet big when the other players aren't. Otherwise, everyone just goes up or down together."

If another player wins some big bets early, you may have to reassess your position earlier than the last five hands.

"He should be in first place going into the last hand, or in the first two if two players advance," says Curtis. "If you're behind other people, you have to count on crazy things happening."

DEAR JOHN: *On April 22, you suggested that craps players should not lay odds on the don't pass bet, as it seems to be "watering down your mathematical edge." However, you never have to risk an odds bet on the come-out roll, where a don't better is most vulnerable. Therefore, by laying maximum odds, you are actually watering down the house advantage, from 1.4 percent to 0.6 percent. A bettor who normally bets $25 on don't pass will find himself losing less and winning more often by betting $5 on don't pass and laying the maximum odds available ($20 on 4 and 10, $21 on 5 and 9, $24 on 6 and 8).*

– Scott, Schaumburg

Answer: It's a matter of whether the odds are laid *instead* of a portion of the don't come bet, or *in addition* to a fixed wager.

Just as you say, a $25 bettor is better off wagering $5 and laying odds than putting it all on the don't pass line. He limits his exposure to the 1.4 percent house edge to $5, and the rest of his bet is a wash, bringing the overall edge down to 0.6 percent.

However, we have a different issue for a table minimum bettor whose don't pass wager is going to be the same regardless of whether he lays odds. This bettor does not limit his exposure to the house edge by laying odds. He's already at the minimum. And at the time he must decide whether to lay the odds, he's the favorite to win the don't pass bet. Once the danger of the come-out is over, the wager the don't bettor has on the table is better than the odds bet.

AUTHOR'S NOTE: In retrospect, I'm not totally happy with this answer. Scott is correct; a don't bettor plays against a lower house advantage if a portion of his wager is reserved to lay the odds. My answer indirectly addresses a money management issue, rather than a question of percentages: If your bankroll will support bets of only $5 a roll, don't increase to $10, regardless of whether the increase comes in the form of a larger don't pass wager or in laying the odds.

DEAR JOHN: *I am an avid slot machine player and find these devices fascinating and challenging. "Looseness" and "tightness" are relative terms since all machines basically generate reel symbol combinations from a tremendously large pool of random numbers. "Loose" machines can suddenly turn cold and "tight" machines can instantly become hot. The key to slot play is to sample a number of machines in the hope of finding a machine or machines that generate winning symbols at the time of play. Additionally, slots should not be played only with the goal of hitting the jackpot (jackpots do occur but very infrequently), but with the idea of getting small but consistent payouts.*

– James McCall, Chicago

Answer: Your last point is one of the most important for slot players to remember. Every time you play a machine, the odds are long against you hitting the top jackpot. Put some of those smaller payouts away and you'll do much better in the long run.

⧫ 13 ⧫

The Warning Signs
Of Problem Gambling

For most of us, a riverboat casino cruise is a fun few hours, a not-too-expensive day's entertainment.

But sometimes, some gamblers go beyond spending what they can afford to lose, and start chasing their losses, trying to win back what they've lost. Then they chase bigger losses, and then even bigger ones.

That gambler, says Chris Anderson, executive director of the Illinois Council on Problem and Compulsive Gambling, is in trouble.

"The typical profile, and on the riverboat it's much more pronounced, is a person who is a casual, social gambler, who gambles periodically for enjoyment or fun, and something happens in his life, a loss or trauma, some sort of negative experience," says Anderson, a certified counselor and therapist.

If he starts gambling with money he can't afford to lose, the gambler is stepping on a treadmill that's very difficult to get off.

"The person who's chasing has to win it back," says Anderson, himself a recovering compulsive gambler. "He's mentally geared that he has to win his money back. Some chase short-term. They lose it and get hold of themselves, or they win it back and say 'that's that, I'll never do that again.'

"The kind of people who get in trouble are the ones who start chasing their chase losses. It becomes a repetitive cycle. And if they don't have money, there's credit, credit card machines, cash advances, markers, they borrow from friends.

"Fifty percent of compulsive gamblers cross the line into illegal activities—bad checks, theft and fraud."

When most compulsive gamblers in the Midwest were horse players or sports bettors, a problem usually was years in the making, according to Anderson. Now he measures in months from the first time a compulsive player steps into a casino until the problem is apparent.

Also, more women are becoming compulsive gamblers.

"Women call for help sooner than men," says Anderson. "In the past women have not had the degree of financial damage men have because they've not had access to as much money. That's changing. We had a call from a woman from out of state who's making $80,000 a year. She says she's losing everything she's making."

Anderson says that, unfortunately, most compulsive gamblers have to hit bottom before the seek help. He names a few things to look for:

"A change in cash flow. Is there a secrecy about money? Have sleeping habits changed? Is he sleeping more, can't sleep, is he restless in sleep? Are there a lot of secret phone calls? Especially in sports betting, there are calls to the bookies and tout sheets. Has he taken out a second mortgage or bank loans? Does he have a lot of credit cards or cash advances?

"With a drug addiction, you can see it. With a compulsive gambler, even when he's in the desperation stage, you wouldn't see it unless you knew what to look for."

If you have a gambling problem, or think you know someone who is a compulsive gambler, please call the council at (800) GAMBLING or Gambler's Anonymous at (312) 346-1588

➳ 14 ⟡
Slot Machine Rules:
Read Them or Weep

For some slot players, it's the stuff of recurring nightmares. Others don't even know what's happening—until it's too late.

You push the button or pull the handle. The reels spin. A jackpot symbol pops up, then another, and another. Your heart starts racing as you look for the top jackpot. Is it $1,000? $10,000? More?

Out of the machine comes … nothing?

Another player has failed to play maximum coins, and on this particular machine failed to activate all the payout combinations.

And it all could have had a happier ending if only the player had taken a minute to understand the machine.

"The most important thing to tell anyone is to read the glass," says Kathleen McLaughlin, director of slot operations at the Hollywood Casino in Aurora. "That explains to you everything you need to know. State regulations require machines to be self-explanatory."

Most slot machines here take either up to three coins or up to two. On some, called multipliers, all winning combinations pay something, no matter how many coins are played. However, there's usually a bonus on the top jackpot for playing maximum coins—for example, a combination that pays 250 coins on the first coin in and 500 on the second coin might pay 2,000 on the third.

On the other type, called buy-a-pays, each coin activates a set of symbols. You might activate bars on the first coin, sevens on the second and special jackpot symbols on the third, for example. Or there might be three paylines instead of one, with each coin activating a separate payline.

"You also have to watch to make sure each coin registers," says Don Wren, slot performance manager at Harrah's Joliet. "You might have one coin in and two jammed. You have to make sure all three registered."

At any machine, it's best to play maximum coin. It's also important to play at a comfortable level. If you can't play the maximum at a machine that takes up to three $1 tokens, move to a two-$1 machine. If you can't play two $1 tokens, play a three-quarter machine, or a two-quarter machine.

For the player who insists on playing one coin, Wren says, "Play a one-line machine. The chance of hitting several small paying combinations on different lines of a three-line machine are so much greater, you don't want to play one coin on them."

Keenan Wright, slot director at the Empress in Joliet, would steer single-coin players to the multipliers.

"On these machines, you will win something on every symbol," Wright says. "You'll win back according to what you put in."

The number of coins in will not affect what combinations appear. The random number generator that governs each machine runs continuously and sets a combination for each pull independent of the number of coins played.

"It's a totally random event," Wright says. "There's nothing in the machine to separate winning combinations according to number of coins played. I've spent hours talking to players on that one."

One type of machine that should never be played with less than maximum coins is the linked progressive. On progressives, a percentage of all the coins played goes into a big jackpot that continuously increases until hit. But only those who play the maximum are eligible to win.

Says Wren, "There's no reason to play a progressive without maximum coins. Just look at that top jackpot and think how it would feel to miss it because of one coin."

❧ 15 ❦
Explaining Video Poker: How Cards Are Dealt

A shuffle through the Gaming mailbag:

DEAR JOHN: *I play video poker at the casinos. I had a possible straight. I needed to eliminate one of two cards. Would the next card drawn appear no matter what position the card was on the screen? Or would one card appear if I eliminated the card in position one and a different card appear if I eliminated the card in position five?*

– Elaine Procento, Hoffman Estates

Answer: In *Slot Machine Mania*, Dwight and Louise Crevelt explain that when the hand is dealt, the program actually distributes two five-card hands at once. It's as if each of the five spots holds a two-card stack. If you discard card No. 1, it will be replaced by the second card in the stack on spot No. 1. So yes, you would get different cards if your discard was at spot No. 5 instead of No. 1.

Don't worry about it too much, though. The distribution still is random. And this program should stop you from second-guessing yourself in the common situation of holding one of two or more high cards in a Jacks or Better game. If, for example, you hold a Jack in spot No. 1 and discard an Ace in spot No. 4, and a second Ace is drawn at No. 4, that does not mean you'd have had a winner if you'd held the first Ace. You'd have drawn the card stacked behind the Jack instead.

Dwight Crevelt, who has worked as a programmer on video poker machines, also has written a follow-up book called *Video Poker Mania,* with playing tips.

DEAR JOHN: *Are the credit and pull handles on slot machines on the same cycle? It seems whenever I let credits build up and push "Max Bet" I have bad luck. Is this just a coincidence?*

– Carolyn Dowis, Sherman, Ill.

Answer: I know the feeling—sometimes when I'm in a cold streak I switch to pulling the handle myself. But yes, it's a coincidence. There is just one random number generator governing the reel combinations, and it makes no difference whether you hit the button or pull the handle.

DEAR JOHN: *In craps, I notice every once in a while someone will ask for a "buy," then a chip is placed in a certain place. Can you explain how this works, and does it improve one's odds? How many numbers does it cover?*

– William Sulich, Oak Lawn

Answer: Buy bets work the same as place bets, except that you pay a 5 percent commission on the buys in return for having the bet pay at true odds. You can buy or place any of the point numbers—4, 5, 6, 8, 9 and 10. If that number is rolled before a 7 you win.

Place bets pay off at 7-6 on 6 or 8; 7-5 on 5 or 9, and 9-5 on 4 or 10. Buy bets pay at correct odds of 6-5 on 6 or 8; 3-2 on 5 or 9, and 2-1 on 4 or 10. Taking into account the commission, the player improves his odds by buying rather than placing the 4 or 10. On the other numbers, the house edge on place bets already is less than the 5 percent commission to buy.

❧ 16 ❧
Know When to Hold 'Em:
Blackjack Basic Strategy

The game of blackjack and I were not always friends.

For a couple years while living in the West, I played in a regular poker game. One of the guys occasionally would call blackjack and deal twice through the deck. It was a good way for the dealer to build his chips, for none of the rest of us had the slightest idea what we were doing.

Casino blackjack? Forget it. The slots or the roulette wheel held more allure my first few visits to Vegas.

The turning point came some years ago before a planned trip to Las Vegas. This time, I decided to go prepared, and bought my first books on gambling. There I discovered basic strategy, developed through analysis of millions of computer generated hands.

Played well, blackjack becomes a game of skill in a casino full of games of chance. There are minor differences among versions of basic strategy by different experts, but all agree on most plays. And the results are dramatic. Basic strategy cuts the house edge to half a percent in an average six- or eight-deck game such as those common in the Midwest.

Compare that with the more than 5 percent edge the house has over someone who plays a never-bust strategy, or over someone who plays dealer's rules, always hitting 16 and under regardless of the dealer's face-up card. Players who have no consistent strategy may fare even worse.

For a solid basic strategy player, the proper plays to hit, stand, double down or split pairs are automatic. They became automatic for me when I dealt myself thousands of hands before that Vegas trip. Others have learned practicing on a computer. Either way, it's worth the effort.

The most common decision a player has to make is whether to hit or stand on a hard total—a hand in which there is not an Ace being used as an 11. An Ace-6 is a soft 17; an Ace-10-6 is a hard 17.

The basic plays for hard totals in a multiple-deck game are detailed below. These won't work every time, and sometimes you'll be frustrated when you see someone else winning while breaking every rule in the book. But these are the best percentage plays. Let making the right play, regardless of result, be its own reward, and in the long run you'll beat the dealer more often.

8 and under: Always hit.

9: Double down—that is, double your original bet after your first two cards and receive only one more card—when the dealer's up-card is a 3, 4, 5 or 6. Hit against a 2 or a 7 and above.

10: Double when the dealer shows a deuce through 9; hit against a 10 or Ace.

11: Double down against anything except an Ace. In a single-deck game, double against the Ace, too.

12: Hit against a 2, 3 or 7 and above. Stand against a 4, 5 or 6.

13 through 16: Hit against a dealer's 7 and above; stand against a 2 through 6. Many players seem to hit the wall at 16 and stand regardless of the dealer's up-card. But that 16 is a loser unless the dealer busts, and the dealer will make 17 or better nearly 80 percent of the time with a 7 or higher showing. The risk of busting by hitting 16 is outweighed by the likelihood you'll lose if you stand.

17 through 21: Always stand.

❧ 17 ❧
Hard Strategy for Betting
Soft Hands in Blackjack

Sometimes it seems the betting public just doesn't get it when it comes to soft hands—those in which an ace is used as an 11—in blackjack.

They may know that the Ace also can be used as a 1 if the next card drawn so dictates, but many players can't quite seem to translate that into a logical playing strategy.

A couple months ago aboard Harrah's Northern Star, a player to my right started with Ace-5—a soft 16—against a dealer's 6. He agonized over his next move and signaled to stand. The dealer asked if he was sure, and the player looked uncertain.

I normally don't give unsolicited advice at the table—this column is the place for that—but I couldn't resist. "You can't hurt that hand," I said, whereupon, with a resigned look, he signaled for a hit. He drew a 5 for 21.

Things don't always work out that well, but there really is nothing you can draw that would hurt a soft 16, or many other soft hands. The worst you wind up with is a hand that could win only by the dealer busting—the same situation as standing on the soft 16.

Just as with the hard totals detailed last week, there is a method called basic strategy that gives the best percentage play for every soft total against any given dealer face-up card. These won't win every hand, but in the long run, playing with the percentages is the way to go.

Here's an overview of basic strategy for soft totals in the multiple-deck games you'll find in the Chicago area:

Ace, Ace: Always split; that is, place a second bet equal to the first and use each Ace as the first card in a new hand. On split Aces, you will get only one more card on each hand. If the house gives you the option of splitting again if you draw another Ace, do so.

Ace, 2; Ace, 3: Double down against a 5 or 6; hit against all other dealer up-cards.

Ace, 4; Ace, 5: Double against a 4, 5 or 6; hit against all else.

Ace, 6: Double down against a 3 through 6; hit against 2 and against 7 and above. This is the most misplayed hand in blackjack. People who understand that the dealer always stands on 17 and that the player always stands on hard 17 seem to think 17 is a good hand, but the dealer must bust for 17 to win. If the dealer does not bust, the best 17 can do is tie. By hitting soft 17, you have a chance to improve it by drawing an Ace, 2, 3 or 4; turn it into a hard 17, losing nothing, by drawing a 10, Jack, Queen or King, or hurt it by drawing 5, 6, 7, 8 or 9. You either improve or don't hurt the hand with 8 of 13 cards, and all you're really giving up is a chance to tie a 17.

Ace, 7: Hit against 9, 10 or Ace; double down against 3, 4, 5 or 6; stand against 2, 7 or 8. That soft 18 isn't as strong as it may seem. The average winning hand in blackjack is 19. In the long run, computer simulations have shown it to be a slightly better risk to hit soft 18, and accept that sometimes you'll ruin a winning hand, than to stand against the 9, 10 or Ace.

Ace, 8; Ace, 9: Stand.

Ace, 10: You have blackjack. Congratulations, and collect your 3-2 payoff.

✤ 18 ✤

More Blackjack Advice:
Splitting and Insurance

A few months ago, Gaming received a letter from a reader asking for an opinion on a blackjack system. The system itself was badly flawed, but particularly striking were the closing items: "Never double down, never split pairs, never take insurance."

That's terrible advice, at least in regard to doubling down and splitting pairs. Along with paying 3-2 on blackjack, allowing players to double down and split pairs in favorable situations are ways the house gives back most of the advantage it gains by winning all the hands the player busts, even if the dealer busts too.

The key is identifying those favorable situations. In the last two columns covering basic strategy for hard totals and soft totals, we've covered most double down situations. Following is a basic strategy for splitting pairs in a common multiple-deck game, in which players are not allowed to doubling down after splitting pairs:

Ace, Ace: Always split.

2,2; 3,3: Split when the dealer shows a 4, 5, 6 or 7; otherwise, hit.

4,4: Never split. An 8 is a much stronger building block than a 4. Just hit.

5,5: Never split. Double down when the dealer's up-card is a 2 through 9.

6,6: Split against 3, 4, 5 or 6. Hit against all others.

7,7: Split against 2 through 7. Hit against 8 through Ace.

8,8: Always split. When the dealer shows a 9, 10 or Ace, splitting is a defensive measure because 16 is such an awful hand. There will be times you'll hit 10s for two 18s and still lose both hands. But you'll lose a little less in the long run if you split rather than play the 16.

9,9: Split against 2 through 6 and against 8 and 9. Stand against 7, 10 and Ace. Because 10s, Jacks, Queens and Kings all count as 10, that is the most common card value in the deck. You're taking that into account when you stand against a 7 but split against an 8. If the dealer has a 10 down, a 7 becomes a 17, which loses to your 18 without a split. But 8 becomes an 18, which ties your hand, and 9 becomes a 19, which beats you if you don't split. You'll do a little better by splitting, rather than standing, against 8 and 9.

10,10: Never split. Don't get greedy and mess up a hand that's going to win most of the time.

The last remaining major blackjack option to cover is insurance. When the dealer's face-up card is an Ace, the dealer will ask if anyone wants insurance. Insurance bets, which pay 2-1 if the dealer has a 10-value card face down to complete a blackjack, may be made for half the original bet.

If you have a blackjack, you may take insurance by calling "even money." The insurance bet of half your original wager cancels out the 3-2 bonus on blackjack, and you are paid even money on your original wager, regardless of the dealer's down-card. If you have bet $10, for example, you're dealt a blackjack and the dealer shows an Ace, you may choose to give up your chance at a $15 payoff if the dealer doesn't have a blackjack. Instead, you take an "even money" $10 payoff rather than risk getting nothing.

Many dealers advise insuring a blackjack, but in the long run it's a bad bet unless you're counting cards and know there is an unusually high concentration of 10-values among cards remaining to be played. Insurance would be an even proposition if the player won one of every three insurance bets, or 33.3 percent. But only 30.8 percent of cards are 10s. Avoid insurance.

❦ 19 ❦
Learn When to Walk Away,
When to Split on Empress II

On the third deck of Empress II, where a single blackjack table and one craps table stand near the tables and chairs set up for snack bar customers, the beginners start to gather.

"You move in here," a middle-aged woman in red and black tells a younger man in a windbreaker. "I'm not really that interested."

At that, it's time for David Stewart, an Empress gaming supervisor, to go to work

"No, you have to play," he tells the woman. "You walked up here (to the no-gaming third level), now you have to play."

He pauses, then, with a smile, continues, "There's room enough for everybody."

It's Stewart's job, and the job of other gaming supervisors, to make the customers comfortable as they learn to play at the instructional tables aboard Empress II. There are lessons in blackjack and craps at 9:30 a.m., 12:30 p.m. and 3:30 p.m. each Monday, Wednesday and Friday.

It's a tried-and-true concept. Many Las Vegas casinos offer gaming instructional tables. In Illinois, the main hold-up has been space. The Illinois Gaming Board does not allow riverboat casinos to open gaming devices to the public anywhere other than on board the boats.

The opening of its second boat gave Empress the space necessary to conduct the sessions on board. No money changes hands. On this day, the crowd hits 18 at its peak to observe Stewart demonstrating the basics.

Blackjack is first. Stewart explains how to place a bet, hand signals for hitting and standing, how to double down, how to split pairs. He deals some practice hands, picking cards out of the deck to demonstrate specifics.

Then it's time for questions. "Can one Ace be an 11 and another a 1," asks an older, sandy-haired man. (Yes, although if they're your first two cards, you might want to split, Stewart tells him.) The man in the windbreaker wonders about the 3-2 bonus for 21. (Only on a blackjack—a two-card 21.) The sandy-haired man pulls a basic strategy card out of his pocket, then asks what it means by soft hands. (Hands in which an Ace is used as an 11.)

They're beginners' questions, and Stewart appreciates them.

"The ones who have questions lighten it up for everyone else," he says later. "One of them will say, 'I wondered about that, but I didn't know how to ask the question.'"

After about 15 minutes, everyone moves over to craps. With its wider variety of bets, Stewart will spend about 40 minutes here.

The advice is sound—he doesn't stick to bets in the casino's favor. He points out the Big 6 and Big 8, which pay even money if the 6 or 8 come up before a 7. "But instead of betting $5 here, why not bet $6 here instead," he says as he moves chips to the boxes to place the 6 and 8. "Here it pays 7-6, so why bet it there?"

Finally, it's time for practice. An older woman rolls a 4, then a 7. "See what happens," says Stewart. "Yeah, you win," jokes the lady in red and black. "No," he says, *"they* do," and he waves around the room.

When it's over, the customers head for the gaming decks. Stewart says he sees some of his pupils at the tables later.

"One day I saw two people who had never played before in the VIP lounge playing quarters (green $25 chips)," he said. "I asked if they might like to start at a table with a lower limit. They said said, 'It doesn't matter.'

"An education costs money no matter what school, right?"

AUTHOR'S NOTE: Though Empress no longer offers this service, I include this July, 1994 column as an example of the kinds of things you can expect from casino gaming lessons.

❧ 20 ❧
Playing With Slot Card
Saves Jackpot Winner

A shuffle through the Gaming mailbag:

DEAR JOHN: *Sometimes, when a player hits a big slot machine jackpot, it's paid by an attendant instead of by the machine. What happens if the player thinks the machine has broken, since it's not spitting out any coins? What if the player walks away? Is the jackpot lost?*

— Sue, Lombard

Answer: If the player has been using a slot club card, he or she may be in luck. Don Wren, slot performance manager at Harrah's Joliet, says players have walked away from hand-paid jackpots twice since Harrah's opened in Illinois last year. One jackpot was lost, but the other player was playing with a Harrah's Gold Card. Wren says Harrah's was able to determine via computer records who hit the jackpot, and later tracked down the winner at home.

DEAR JOHN: *In Vegas, the dealer hits soft 17. In Peoria (and in Joliet and Aurora), dealer stands. Which is to my advantage?*

— Lee Yotto, Danville

Answer: It's to the player's advantage for the house to stand on all 17s for the same reason the player should hit soft 17. An Ace, 2, 3 or 4 improves the hand, a 10, Jack, Queen or King leaves it the same. So 8 of every 13 cards either improve soft 17 or leave it no worse. And even if one of the other five cards is drawn, the dealer who hits soft 17 still has a chance to make his hand with another draw.

In *The World's Greatest Blackjack Book*, Lance Humble estimates the house gains an additional two-tenths of a percent edge when the dealer hits soft 17.

You can find the game dealt either way in Las Vegas. On the face-up games with four decks or more on the Strip, it's most common for the dealer to stand on all 17s. In most single- and double-deck games and in most games in downtown Las Vegas, the dealer hits soft 17.

DEAR JOHN: *I found your columns on blackjack strategy very interesting. I hope to memorize all the basic plays, but I have a trip to Atlantic City coming up soon, and I was wondering if you had a simpler strategy that I could learn in a hurry.*

– Tom, Chicago

Answer: Here's a stripped-down version of basic strategy that loses some of the fine points, but will give you the best percentage play most of the time: Stand on hard 12 through 16 when the dealer shows a 2 through 6; hit hard 12 through 16 when the dealer shows 7 through Ace; always hit soft 13 through 17; stand on 17 through 21, except soft 17; always split Aces and 8s; double 10 and 11 when the dealer shows a 2 through 9.

Wondering why a hit isn't called for on soft 12? That's a pair of Aces, which you always split.

DEAR JOHN: *Please help! I enjoy gambling very much, but I am not a big enough gambler to defray the cost of traveling to Las Vegas, nor do I like flying very much. The riverboat casinos are always too crowded.*

This winter, I drove eight hours to an Indian reservation near Traverse City, Mich., which had the games I wanted (blackjack, roulette and craps), but the drive was very strenuous. Casino personnel informed me that during the more appealing weather months, they also are very crowded. My problem lies in locating a casino that is closer to Chicago and has roulette and craps tables. Those in Wisconsin that I'm aware of have only blackjack and slots.

– Dale Muller, Chicago

Answer: Your best bet to find all those games in less crowded conditions is to play midweek in the daytime on the riverboats.

Crowded conditions have eased considerably since the Empress and Harrah's opened their second boats. I've found no problems in getting to a table playing at those times.

As you've found, the standard games at Wisconsin casinos are blackjack, bingo, slots and video poker, and some don't offer blackjack. None offers roulette or craps.

If you wish to look for information on casinos elsewhere in the Midwest, the best source I've found is the *Casino/Resort, Riverboat and Fun Book Guide,* published by Casino Vacations, P.O. Box 703, Dania, Fla. 33004. Updated yearly, it lists every casino in the United States as of publication date, with phone numbers, games offered and other casino features.

AUTHOR'S NOTE: The guide referred to in the last answer still is updated yearly, but now is called the *American Casino Guide.*

❧ 21 ❧

High Rollin' on the River:
Comps for Big Spenders

Cheryl Jewell's recent homecoming also was an opportunity, a chance to impress 110 of Harrah's Joliet's best customers.

"Last weekend was unbelievable," said Jewell, a Harrah's casino host who had just returned from guiding the group to Harrah's Lake Tahoe, where she had gotten her start in the industry. "It gives us a chance to show what we can do. We have a five-star hotel, there are shows, live entertainment, seven restaurants on the property.

"This is our chance to wow 'em. We want 'em to be our apostles."

As long as there have been casinos, there have been complimentaries—perks given to keep the customers coming back. Comps can be anything from a free soft drink to someone playing a quarter slot machine to trips, parties and restaurant meals for high-end players.

In the Chicago area, Harrah's, the Empress and Hollywood all find themselves developing a clientele of high-rolling regulars—though not the same kind of high-roller who bets tens of thousands per hand in the baccarat pits of Las Vegas. Here, the player who bets $100, $50, even $25 a hand stands out.

"The high end here is not necessarily the same as the high end in Vegas or Atlantic City," said Vic Kastil, marketing director of the Hollywood Casino in Aurora. "These days in Nevada, before a player is offered room, food and beverage, it takes a $10,000 line; that is, the player must show he has the opportunity to lose or win $10,000. Here that number is reduced dramatically. We extend ourselves way, way below that figure. The $200-$300, $400, $1,000 player has a chance to be considered a top quality player."

Kastil says that's because the casino's cost for high-end comps is much lower here. Instead of several nights in a hotel room or suite, shows, all meals and beverages, the high-end player on the riverboats is looking at an evening out, with admission, valet parking, dinner in one of the pavilion restaurants and sometimes a show. All on the house.

Len Pascarelli, marketing director at the Empress in Joliet, says his facility has a few extras. "We provide a boarding lounge. It has a parlor environment where they can rest and relax," he said. "We have our gourmet restaurant (the Alexandria Club) with a full wine list—a complete wine cellar, really.

"We have recognition parties for birthdays and special days. We take them to skyboxes at Soldier Field and Comiskey Park. We have our off-track betting facility. All on a complimentary basis, of course."

Access to all that starts with the bettor's play being rated. And that's done with the same card that 25-cent players use at the slot machines. At Harrah's, it's the Gold Card; the Empress Club has its Platinum card, and Hollywood starts its players off with the Screen Test Card, though at the high end players quickly pass their screen tests and move to the Marquee Card.

At the tables, a floor person will take the card to clock the player in, note the buy-in, average bet and length of time played.

Factoring all that together allows the casino to estimate how much it will win from a particular player. The player will win sometimes and lose more than the estimate at other times, but in the long run the percentages hold up. The casino gives a portion of its expected win back in the form of comps.

But, says Kastil, there's something even more important than the perks offered.

"The high end of the business is a no-gimmick business," he said. "The degree of personal attention, that's what the high-end player focuses on. They realize that when they come here they're going to receive personal attention that they certainly don't receive in other jurisdictions. They don't have the time. They have 3,000 rooms, 4,000-room hotels, hundreds of table games, thousands of slots to look after.

"By personal attention we mean the customer gets a complimentary dinner, a big 'Hello, how are you, can we take care of your valet parking, please be our guest for dinner.' That same person in Las Vegas might not get a cup of coffee."

Personal attention is where the casino hosts, people like Harrah's Jewell, come in.

When the hosts spot a new high-end player, Jewell said, "We wait until there's a break in the shoe. We already know the first name (because of the rating card). Then I'll say, 'Let me introduce myself. If there's anything we can do for you, make reservations on the boat or in the restaurant, let me know.' Then we send a follow-up letter.

"Whether I know the first name or last name, I greet people by name. I meet maybe 1,000 people a day, and I try to remember all the first names. If I say 'Hi John' and it's Jim, I'll smile and make a little joke, say, 'At least I got the first part right.'

❧ 22 ❧
Even the Low Rollers
Should Play the Comp Card

Most of us will never have a casino send a limousine for us, or comp us to dinner and wine at its high-end restaurant, or fly us to a distant resort.

That doesn't mean they don't want to keep us coming back. Comps are for the average player, too, those who play the quarter slot machines or play at the $5 minimum tables.

The key is to sign up for the player rating cards offered at all the riverboat casinos—the Platinum Card at the Empress, the Gold Card at Harrah's and the Screen Test or Marquee Card at the Hollywood. There is no fee to sign up, and the benefits start immediately, even before you've inserted the card into a magnetic reader on a slot machine or handed it to a floorperson at the tables.

"For the average player, it starts with having the Platinum Card," said Len Pascarelli, marketing director of the Empress. "Just for having the card, they receive complimentary boarding, discount valet parking and a 15 percent discount at our food and beverage outlets.

"For using the card, and that means inserting and removing it, these individuals upon request may be offered access to our food amenities. Soon we'll be opening our Marrakech Food Court that will be available to a player of this caliber.

Frequently, there are invitations to special events and access to promotions not available to those who don't sign up for the cards. A recent Empress Club mailing to Platinum Card holders included coupons for a free turkey buffet and a free T-shirt to coincide with the casino's Christmas in July promotion. Harrah's Gold Card customers recently were treated to a spin of a wheel for prizes including free boarding, gift shop items, restaurant vouchers and $20 in cash.

"Those who obtain and use a Gold Card may receive free tickets, valet parking, special announcements, gifts, perhaps entries into player sweepstakes, invitations to other events, such as boxing and player parties," said Harrah's marketing director Gaye Gullo. "The card in itself also provides discounts in the gift shops and discounts at other Harrah's."

At Empress and Harrah's, customers must check with the club to find out what comps their play has earned them. At Hollywood, where customers move up from the Screen Test card to the Marquee Card as they play more, the system is the same on the tables.

But on the slots, Hollywood players can get readings of their point totals at any time, and a table is issued telling players how many points it takes for specific comps.

"We figure the customer responds when he knows exactly what to expect and can keep track on a daily basis." said marketing director Vic Kastil. "It's almost like frequent flyer miles," One thing we factor in is the amount of visits, the frequency. The $5, $10, $15 player who displays a degree of loyalty is going to be rewarded. We can't reward them on a daily basis in the gourmet restaurant, but they will be invited from time to time to the restaurant and various shows.

"And we have the buffet downstairs, cruise tickets, parking. We let them know we appreciate their business. If we see them here on a regular basis, we'll take care of them."

Gullo says Harrah's has studied creating a point system, but that either way, the customer will be pleased.

"We're a national brand so the first step is creating a program so that the Gold Cards have value at all the properties," Gullo said. "If our Joliet customers use our card in Las Vegas, Harrah's Las Vegas may send an offer for free rooms.

"In terms of developing a point system, we've not reached a consensus on that yet. But I can assure the customer that in terms of the comparative nature of the product, we're all on the same competitive plane. They may define the matrix at Hollywood, but the same level of play would lead to the same benefit here."

Gamblers who are used to playing in Las Vegas but are new to the boats, people who are used to requesting meal comps after playing for a while even if they're not a rated player at a particular casino, will find they'll be taken care of on the riverboats, as well, usually with a suggestion that they sign up for a card.

"We get requests rather frequently from experienced gamers," said Pascarelli of the Empress, "and that's a good thing. We want to appeal to the experienced casino player as well as the first-timer. We do seek to offer the first-time customer some level of recognition to expose him to our amenities to encourage him to return to us rather that our competition."

AUTHOR'S NOTE: Slot clubs, player rating cards and specific comp offers are continually evolving. Many of the details have changed since this column first appeared on August 5, 1994. Harrah's and Empress both switched to systems that allow slot players to see their point totals, and rewards now include cash back. The basics are the same, however. If you're going to play anyway, sign up for a card, use it and you'll get back a little extra.

❧ 23 ❧

Casino Insider Offers
A Guide to Freebies

You're playing blackjack in Las Vegas, and it's about time for a dinner break. You're going to want a glass of wine with your meal. What do you do?

If you're Max Rubin, you order the wine at the gaming table, where all it will cost is a tip to the cocktail waitress, then you take it into the restaurant with you.

But then Rubin is a comp wizard, with an insider's knowledge of the casino industry, and he plays angles that have never even dawned on the rest of us. The wine ploy won't work in Illinois, where it's illegal to give free alcoholic beverages on casino cruises. But that's just a warmup, anyway.

"Are you a player?" Rubin said by phone from his Las Vegas home. "Isn't free stuff great?"

In *Comp City: A Guide to Free Las Vegas Vacations,* Rubin lets gamblers in on the secrets of how to get their share of free stuff—and more. The book is geared to visitors to Vegas, where casinos give away more than $500,000 a day in comps. But most of his methods can be applied almost anywhere.

"The same principles apply everywhere, except in Canada," he said. "The Canadians won't comp you anything. They don't need to. It's already standing room only."

At $39.95 (from Huntington Press, 800-244-2224), the 296-page hardcover isn't cheap. But a little applied comp wizardry can make up the cost.

The first step toward anything from a buffet comp for a $5 player to room, food, beverage, shows, limo rides, greens fees, even airfare for a higher roller is to learn basic strategy in blackjack. There are tips for those who play slots and other games, but the best comp plays are in blackjack, where odds are fluid, depending on the skill of the player.

"Most places in Vegas give back 20 to 40 percent of the expected win—not the actual win," Rubin said.

That's where comp wizardry begins, for the casino expects to win more—and does against most players—than the basic strategy player actually loses. Where the casino might estimate a 2 percent house advantage, a basic strategy player in a six-deck game with a good set of rules can cut that to about half a percent. At that level, the player may receive comps worth more than 100 percent of actual losses.

At that point, Rubin is just getting started, with tips on how to make your average bet look bigger than it really is to qualify for bigger comps. He tells how to limit losses by finding a slow table and making it even slower. And he has advice on what to look for in a casino boss.

The result is goods and services for 10 cents in casino losses on the dollar, says Rubin, who adds a warning that natural fluctuations mean that sometimes the buffet comp will cost many times its value in losses. At other times, the player will win, and the net is lots of comps at little cost.

Naturally, players aren't the only people interested in his methods.

"Since the book came out, I've been hired as a consultant at two casinos," said Rubin, who has worked as everything from dishwasher to dealer to casino executive, and has been a professional gambler. "It's such a new industry, the people in it don't understand much about their own industry."

Perhaps his best tip is his simplest: Ask.

"Most people don't even know what's available. They don't ask in the first place," he said. "They're shy, they don't think they've played enough.

"But if you're going to play anyway, go ahead and get the good stuff."

❧ 24 ❧

Gaming Industry Deals
Women Into the Game

When Rosemarie Cook became a table games supervisor in Atlantic City in 1980, she wasn't quite sure what her customers expected.

"It took a while for guests to get used to the fact there were women there, too," says Cook, now director of casino operations at the Hollywood Casino in Aurora. "My first management position at Bally's Park Place was in the baccarat pit. It took a little while for the players to get used to the fact they had to deal with a woman.

"The player would say, 'I want to speak to the boss,' and I'd say, 'That's me, I am the boss.' And they'd look and say, 'Oh? Oh. OK.'"

Today's casinos no longer are smoke-filled, male-dominated environments where a woman's place is as a cocktail waitress. From dealers to high-ranking executives, women have become an important part of the industry.

Sue Reyes, the human resources manager at Harrah's Joliet, says the growth of Atlantic City casinos starting in 1978 was a catalyst for bringing women into the business.

"New Jersey was highly regulated, and the casinos needed to make the EEO (Equal Employment Opportunity) stats," says Reyes, who has worked in human resources and labor relations since joining Harrah's in 1980. "To meet the state and city requirements, they needed women at the supervisory level or above, and they had to come from Nevada. That's where all the experienced people were. The first wave of supervisors all came from Nevada for the promotion opportunities."

"The biggest obstacle women had through the '80s was that there were very few mentors. There weren't that many of us. Women created our own network. All the women working in casinos knew each other. Even if you didn't work together, you met or heard about them through friends."

One of the women Reyes met was Gaye Gullo, who started as a bus greeter at the Tropicana (now TropWorld) in 1984, then moved to Harrah's in 1985.

At the Trop, it was her job to greet tour buses and hand out coupon books. She heard a few untoward remarks in those days, but says she handled it with a sense of humor.

"The only time anyone ever touched me, his mother was in the seat in front of him," Gullo says, "and she turned around and cracked him and told him to behave himself."

Gullo, now the marketing director at Harrah's Joliet, says the movement of women up through the organization picked up steam after Atlantic City had been open to gaming for several years.

"There was a learning curve for six or seven years," she says. "Women would start in a clerical job, then supervisory, then management and get that under our belts and move up though the ranks."

Judi Talbot, the senior director of support services at the Empress in Joliet, took a different route to the casino world. She came to the Empress almost three years ago from the hotel industry.

"The hotel industry also has been very male dominated," she says. "The two industries are very similar. As a matter of fact, it's a challenge. It instills a certain motivation because of the challenge.

"We have female shift managers. Quite a few women are in table games operations. They're on the floor, running the day-to-day operations. As long as she performs well, meets or exceeds standards, shows quality in becoming a dealer and working her way to upper management positions, I'd certainly not discourage anybody."

That's much different from 1978, when Cook started as a dealer at Resorts International, the first Atlantic City casino to open. Then there were few women bosses to show her the ropes.

"When I started dealing at Resorts, the people standing behind me were all men," says Cook. "In 60,000 square feet of casino, there were only five women supervisors, and they were all at the first level."

But Cook wouldn't trade that experience at the bottom level for anything.

"My advice to a young woman would be to take an entry level position," she says. "There's no background like that. Work the position, get a feel for it, get a feel for gaming. Spend some time as a dealer. Don't try to advance too fast."

❧ 25 ❧
Elgin's New Riverboat
Plays With a Full Deck

After more than two years of riverboat gambling in the Chicago area, customers might think they know pretty much what to expect. Peter Simon promises something different.

"We didn't build a boat and try to put a casino inside," says Simon, a partner in the Grand Victoria river casino due to open this fall in Elgin. "We designed a casino and built a boat around it."

The casino Simon wanted built, which he says will open "as close to Oct. 1 as possible," required something different in boat design. Unlike Harrah's, Hollywood and the Empress, which all split their allotted 1,200 gaming positions over two boats, Grand Victoria will open with more than 1,000 slots, 36 blackjack tables, six craps tables and two roulette wheels on one boat.

Almost all those gaming positions will be on a single deck. Other than a few slot machines in the snack bar area of the first deck, everything will be in the second-deck casino that extends nearly 36,000 square feet.

"The point is to try to duplicate the experience people feel when they go to a major land-based casino," says Simon, one of four Nevada Landing partners in the consortium with Hyatt Development Corporation that will run the Elgin operation. "I've been here three years. When we started out in '91 it was two boats, but in the spring of '92 we decided on one boat for a lot of reasons, all of which were visible when you walked through."

Built in Elgin by Chicago Bridge and Iron workers and launched in July, the boat is 400 feet long and 116 feet wide, with a paddlewheel look. Inside, there will be no walls in the casino space. Simon says some areas will be designated as smoke free, but says an ionization system should keep the whole casino comfortable for nonsmokers. "We'll have a complete exchange of air every two minutes," he says. "As you can tell by all the vents, we're trying to make this as much a smoke free environment as possible."

The casino deck is roughly comparable in size to a mid-size Las Vegas hotel casino—not the Mirage or MGM by any means, but only 4,000 square feet smaller than the Flamingo Hilton, 11,000 square feet larger than the Sands and the same size as the Golden Nugget. It takes an enormous boat to hold that casino, and here, too, Grand Victoria is a little different. Whereas Hollywood decided to cope with the narrowness of the Fox River by building two boats that are short stem to stern so they can turn around in the river, but tall with four decks of gaming, Grand Victoria will not turn around. After it heads out on a cruise, it will reverse engines to return.

The boat will dock next to Grand Victoria pavilion, an 83,000-square foot facility with a three-screen movie theater, a sports bar, VIP lounge, banquet facility, steak house, buffet, food court and snack bar.

"Originally we planned a smaller pavilion," Simon says. "We conducted many meetings with local residents and we asked them, 'What do you think downtown Elgin needs to revitalize itself?' After about 20 or 30 meetings, the top three were a movie theater, an upscale restaurant and a nice place to have a drink."

Project manager Joe Faust says all the behind the scenes work is done. He expects to begin installing slot machines and gaming tables in early September. All that leaves Simon confident Grand Victoria can meet its target date, pending Gaming Board approval.

"Even the weather has been on our side," says Simon. "We started out with that terrible winter, but since then it's been dry when we needed it to be dry and rained when we needed it to rain—the day of the launch the river level was at its highest all season."

AUTHOR'S NOTE: This column originally appeared August 26, 1994. Grand Victoria opened in early October, and by mid-1995 had become the gross revenue leader among Illinois casinos.

❧ 26 ❧
Mail Call: Blackjack Odds,
Slot Strategy, Job Advice

A shuffle through the Gaming mailbag:

DEAR JOHN: *My son and I had an argument: Does the house have an edge in blackjack? I say they have an edge, my son thinks otherwise. Please straighten us out.*

— Joseph F. Vancura, Riverside

Answer: Who has the edge depends on the skill of the player, but players who can gain an edge over the house are rare. Against an average player, the house figures it has an edge of about 2 percent; some customers play at a considerably larger disadvantage. Against a player who knows and uses basic strategy, the edge is narrow, about half a percent, more or less depending on rules in the particular casino, but the house still has the advantage.

However, the very few players who know basic strategy, are skilled at counting cards and raise and lower their bets in accordance with the count can have a small edge against the house.

So you and your son are both right, but you're more right than he is, since the house has an edge against 99.9 percent of players.

DEAR JOHN: *Are there chips installed in slot machines that affect the payout? I had an experience with one of the Illinois riverboats where the machine I was playing was winning and I felt real lucky. A few days later I went back to the boat and the machine I was playing, as well as all the other machines of the same type, were turned off. I was upset and called the Illinois Gaming Board when I got home. A few days later I was called back and told the machines were back on, without an explanation. When I went back the machines didn't pay out like they used to. Is there a way they could have "fixed" them?*

– Pam Sabon, no address

Answer: Though it is possible that with Gaming Board approval, the chips governing the payout percentage could have been changed, your experience is well within the normal range of chance. The board requires that over the long term—100,000 to 300,000 plays—each machine pay out not less than 80 percent nor more than 100 percent. In the short term there's room for much wider variation. Almost any machine operating within the legal limits will have short periods during which it pays out 150 percent—more if a big jackpot is hit—and short periods when it pays 50 percent or less. Your best defense is simply to get out quickly when the payouts are low.

DEAR JOHN: *Are roulette wheels being manipulated to stop at a certain spot at a given time, or does the ball randomly land on a certain spot? Once, when I was playing, the wheel stopped, the ball landed and suddenly (as though it had wings), it jumped up and landed on another spot. I have never been able to trust the wheel since.*

– P. Gordon, no address

Answer: The ball takes some odd jumps in roulette, a result of the ball and wheel being spun in opposite directions taken in combination with the design and construction of the wheel. It's all meant to keep the numbers as random as possible. As long as the numbers stay random, the house has a healthy 5.26 percent edge on an American 00 wheel. That's one of the bigger house percentages on table games, and it's in the house interest to keep the game honest. If you suspect otherwise, call the Illinois Gaming Board. Be sure to give specifics as to where you were playing, at what wheel and what happened to make you suspicious.

DEAR JOHN: *I'm currently working as a waitress in a south suburban restaurant. One of my former co-workers attended a gambling school in Indiana. Now she is employed at the Empress as a blackjack dealer. She tells me she makes $45,000 a year. Is this possible?*

– Jenny, no address

Answer: It is possible for a dealer to make $45,000, but it's no sure thing. Dealer's jobs pay minimum wage, $4.25 an hour, and the rest comes from tips. Several months ago, Ed Devlin, then a shift manager with the Hollywood Casino who since has moved, said his dealers were averaging about $15 an hour in tips. That would put the job in the $40,000 range. Other casinos say $10 an hour in tips is more typical.

Dealer jobs are much sought after, and most candidates in the Chicago area do not come from commercial dealers' schools. Empress and Harrah's in Joliet and Hollywood in Aurora all run their own schools and open classes to in-house candidates first. That will be the policy at Grand Victoria in Elgin as well. Your best chance to become a dealer is to take any job in a casino operation—waitress in one of the restaurants would do—and wait to become eligible for the in-house dealers' school.

❧ 27 ❧
Casino Executive Reveals
Science of Marketing Slots

Reached in Las Vegas one recent morning, Frank Scoblete was taking his own advice.

"Right now I'm at the Rio, and I've been playing this same near-100 percent slot machine and getting my breakfast comped every morning," said Scoblete, whose latest book is *Break the One-Armed Bandits* (Bonus Books). "I go play table games in the afternoon, but every morning I come back here and play for breakfast."

Until now, Scoblete's focus has been on table games, with *Beat the Craps Out of the Casino* and *Guerrilla Gambling*. But for *Break the One-Armed Bandits*, he scored a breakthrough that sets his book apart from other slot books on the market. A casino executive, who Scoblete calls "Mr. Handle," agreed to be interviewed about the theory and psychology of the placement of better-paying slots machines.

Not all slots—not even all slots of the same type—pay back at the same percentage. Placing high percentage machines so that the sights and sounds of winners encourage play on low-paying machines has become a science.

"I approached about 30 (casino executives), and most didn't even want to talk to me," said Scoblete. "They're very elusive, leery of publicity, because they see most of it as bad publicity. But one guy was more than happy to talk, because he thinks it'll make more money for the casino, just like blackjack opened up," encouraging more players when books were written suggesting it's a beatable game.

"He just opened up. There are quite a few things I wasn't able to put in the book, serial numbers of actual machines, but in general this is the first time the specific locations of looser machines has been revealed.

"It was a really big coup. Then I had to go write a book around it."

The result is not a pie-in-the-sky, get-rich-quick-book. It's a fun read, with plenty of useful advice on playing the slots. But the book's subtitle, *How to Come Out Ahead When You Play the Slots*, doesn't mean that if you locate a high-paying machine, you're in for instant jackpots. It suggests that using Mr. Handle's information will enable a player to bring the total return, once slot club comps are added, to more than 100 percent.

"Absolutely, they (players) have to use the whole program," said Scoblete. "Through the whole thing, I found no 100 percent payback machines, though there were some at 99 percent."

Scoblete interviewed more than 2,000 slot players, and found that most had no idea where the loose machines were. Many of their beliefs wound up in a chapter called Superstitions, Stories and Statements.

But the unquestioned centerpiece of the book is the interview with Mr. Handle.

"One major revelation is that before, people thought the slots near the table games were loose, and they're tighter than hell," Scoblete said. "There's no real reason for them to be loose—the table players don't want to hear the noise of the coins in the background. It's not going to encourage them to play the slots."

That leads to a tip for those who play on some of the smaller riverboats, which sometimes have row after row of machines, rather than the groupings Scoblete and Mr. Handle describe.

In that situation, says Scoblete, "You probably have to look at the end machines nearest the aisle, and any machine visible from a coffee shop. Definitely stay away from the high-roller table games."

❧ 28 ❧

Multiple-Action Blackjack
Multiplies Urge to Misplay

Advice from other players can be hazardous to your bankroll, especially in a new game like Multiple-Action Blackjack.

A kind of hazy strategy consensus has developed, and many players seem eager to share their views.

Aboard Empress II recently, I asked dealer Lori if most players simply tried not to bust in this game, she remained noncommittal, saying only that "you have to adjust your strategy a little."

That was the cue for a gentleman at my left to explain how it's done. "You have to keep the hand alive, whatever you do," he said. "If you bust, you lose three hands at once. If you keep the hand alive, you have a chance."

I've heard that same advice at a dozen other casinos, and that's the way most players go about business at Multiple-Action, a game developed by the Four Queens in downtown Las Vegas.

Unfortunately, the never-bust strategy actually increases the house edge. The best percentage strategy in Multiple-Action is the same basic strategy used in regular blackjack.

Available in Illinois at Harrah's, Empress and the Par-A-Dice, Multiple-Action gives each player three betting spots. The player is dealt one hand, and the dealer gets a single face-up card that is played with different draws three times. After all players have finished hitting or standing, the dealer draws cards to settle hand No. 1. The dealer then moves the up-card to a second spot, and plays the hand again, then repeats for the third bets.

It's a fascinating game, from the thrill of seeing a blackjack come up with three bets on the table to the agony of watching the dealer then come up with three consecutive face cards on his Ace—as happened to me once at the Tropicana in Las Vegas.

It's also a difficult game, because the temptation to misplay hands is tremendous. Most players do not want to lose three bets at once, so they stand on 12 or higher regardless of the dealer up-card. They hope the dealer will bust one or more hands.

They don't see that it increases their risk to make a shaky strategy decision for the sake of keeping the hand alive.

Look at it this way: If you're dealt 16s against dealer 10s three different times in regular blackjack, you'd hit each one, wouldn't you? You'll make 17 or better about 38 percent of the time. The dealer will bust less than 20 percent. You're better off to risk busting rather than waiting for the dealer.

Those percentages are exactly the same in Multiple-Action.

The possibility of losing three bets at once is an intimidation factor that sinks most Multiple-Action players. At a $5 minimum table, the player who bets all three spots—you are allowed to play either two or three—has at least $15 on the table at once. If you're not willing to risk $15 on a hit/stand decision, you should not be playing Multiple-Action.

Here are a couple other points to consider at Multiple-Action:

Bankroll: You should be prepared to bring to the table at least twice your regular blackjack bankroll. I would not recommend buying in at a $5 table for less than $100, and even then it only takes a couple triple losses to make a serious dent.

Table conditions: Sometimes the house rules at Multiple-Action are significantly worse than at regular blackjack tables in the same casino. If the house allows the player to double down after splits at regular tables but bars this play at Multiple-Action, for example, I'd rather play at a regular table. There's no need to give the house an extra edge.

❧ 29 ❧
Your First Blackjack Move: Picking a Hospitable Table

More than any other casino game offered in Illinois, blackjack combines elements of skill with chance, from choice of hit/stand strategies to money management techniques to, for some, counting cards.

But one blackjack skill that's often overlooked should be applied before you even sit down to play. Choosing a game with favorable table conditions is as important a skill as any other.

When you walk onto a riverboat, you have no choice of rules and conditions—what's on board is what's on board. Still, the smart player will take note of the rules in force at each gaming site, and take that into account when planning excursions. In the case of a particularly unfavorable set of rules, he or she might even avoid the game.

In Las Vegas, comparing conditions is even more important. There, if you encounter an unfavorable set of rules, you can walk from casino to casino until you find a better game. Other parts of Nevada, Mississippi and Atlantic City also offer some chances to comparison shop.

Here are some common blackjack variations, some that favor the player, some that favor the house:

Number of decks: All other conditions being the same, the fewer the decks, the better for the player. In Illinois, all games are six- or eight-deckers. Single- and double-deck games are easiest to find in Nevada; Mississippi is another good spot for single-deck.

Dealer hits soft 17: A bad rule for the player. The average winning hand is 19. Hitting soft 17 gives the dealer a chance to improve a so-so hand.

Double down after splitting pairs: Any rule that gives the player more options is good, as long as the player uses it wisely. When the casino allows the player to double after splitting, a slight adjustment to basic strategy is needed. Basic strategy if doubling after splits is allowed is slightly different than the strategy presented in this column a few months ago. If your casino allows doubling after splits, adjust basic strategy as follows:

Split 2,2 and 3,3 if the dealer's up-card is 2 through 7 instead of against 4 through 7; split 4,4 against a dealer's 5 or 6 instead of hitting; split 6,6 against 2 through 6 instead of 3 through 6.

Surrender: Occasionally, you'll find a house that will allow you to surrender half your bet rather than playing out your hand. If the house allows you to do this before the dealer checks his down card for blackjack, it's called early surrender. If, more commonly, the house checks first and collects all bets if the dealer has blackjack, it's late surrender. A good rule for players is to surrender hard 16s—except a pair of 8s—against the dealer's 9, 10 or Ace, and surrender 15 against a 10. Play out all other hands.

Resplitting Aces allowed: It can be maddening to split Aces, only to be dealt another Ace. That 12 wins only if the dealer busts, and almost all casinos limit you to a one-card draw on a split Ace. If the house allows resplitting of Aces, do so.

No dealer hole card: This variation, common on cruise ships, would make no difference if not for a nasty little rule that goes with it. The dealer does not deal himself a second card until the players have completed their hands, and so he does not check for blackjack before players double or split. If the dealer then completes the blackjack, the house takes both bets on doubles and splits. A horrendous rule.

So what's the best set of rules you can expect to find in a package? The Riviera in Las Vegas currently deals a single-deck game in which the dealer stands on all 17s and doubling after splits is allowed. The basic strategy player has about a one-tenth of one percent advantage over the house.

The worst? Well, I once saw a casino on a cruise ship that dealt an eight-deck game with no dealer hole card, no double after splits, no resplitting of pairs. An ugly game, but the captive audience kept the tables busy.

⟐ 30 ⟐
Wheelchair Accessibility
On Riverboat Casinos

A shuffle through the Gaming mailbag:

DEAR JOHN: *My friend says that at a casino she visits in Nevada, they ask her from time to time if she would like to be moved to another table. She is in a wheelchair, as am I. Would the casinos here provide the same kind of service?*

– Name withheld

Answer: Harrah's, the Empress and the Hollywood all say casino employees would be happy to help customers in wheelchairs move to a different table or slot machine. Alan Rosenzweig, director of marketing at Hollywood, said, "Basically, we would provide assistance to anyone who requested it in the form of security officers assisting the customers on request. We're not able to provide a constant escort."

Jim Murphy, the marketing director at the Empress, and Lorraine Klebba, director of public affairs at Harrah's, gave essentially the same answer. "A valet or security person would be happy to push the customer or provide special assistance," said Murphy. Klebba would direct the customer to "a customer safety representative or a gaming host, any Harrah's employee, really."

The bottom line is just to ask if you need assistance. Ask the dealer at your table or the nearest slot host and they'll arrange for someone to help you.

All the riverboats and their pavilions are wheelchair accessible, with ramps and elevators available to take you to any level. All have separate boarding for passengers in wheelchairs or who need assistance. In addition,

Murphy says that wheelchairs are available for loan at the valet area at the Empress, and Klebba points out that all Harrah's tables and slots are designed to be accessible to physically challenged customers. At Hollywood, where the parking garage is a couple blocks from the pavilion, transportation in a trolley equipped with a lift can be arranged from the garage to the front door of the pavilion.

DEAR JOHN: *Why do the video poker and slot machines have to use special coins from the casino? Harrah's, Empress, Hollywood, Silver Eagle all have to have the house money. Yet when I was in Minnesota I used regular quarters. Do the casinos figure that if a gambler has only coins that can only be used on that specific boat and not ashore that the gambler will use up all the coins because they aren't any use anywhere else?*
— Elaine Procento, Hoffman Estates

Answer: You can add Par-A-Dice, Casino Queen, Players, Casino Rock Island, Alton Belle and, when it opens soon, Grand Victoria to your list. Illinois riverboat casinos are required both by state regulations and Illinois Gaming Board rules to operate under a cashless system. Cory Aronovitz, the Gaming Board's legal counsel and interim public information officer, cited two places in the regulations and two in the board's rules in which wagering is limited to electronic cards, chips and tokens that may be used only in the issuing casino.

"It's all based on maintaining the integrity of gaming," Aronovitz said. "The board has worked very hard to protect the integrity of gaming."

Harrah's Klebba says the regulations were written in part so that purchases of tokens could be quantified. When regular U.S. coins are used, the customer can bring any amount from the outside, making an accurate count of what has been purchased and played more difficult.

Use of tokens at denominations smaller than $1 really started spreading with the advent of riverboat gaming in Iowa. Regulations in Iowa at that time limited customers to a maximum $200 in losses per cruise, so a way was needed to quantify just how much play the customer had. If regular coins were used, it would have been difficult to prevent customers from bringing more than $200 in playable coins aboard.

Tribal casinos opened in Minnesota before riverboat gaming began and followed Nevada's long-established policy of using coins in all slot denominations of less than $1.

❧ 31 ❧
Best Bets, Worst Bets:
Playing the Percentages

Casino players decide what games to play and what bets to make for a variety of reasons.

The player who likes to yell and scream and have a lot of action at once probably heads straight for the craps table. Quieter folks who want decisions to make in a game that requires concentration probably play blackjack.

Some prefer the slower pace of roulette, and some prefer not to deal with table etiquette or rules, and head for the slot machines.

But another way to choose a game is to play the percentages. The house edge varies widely between games, and between bets in the same game. Here's a look at where to find the games with the lowest house advantage, along with a couple bets to avoid.

BEST BETS

1. **BLACKJACK, basic strategy player:** In the best six-deck games in Illinois, the basic strategy player can hold the house advantage to about half of 1 percent. The only players in the casino with a better deal are skilled card counters, who can gain a slight edge in blackjack. They're a rare breed, though, because counting cards under today's playing conditions—multiple decks, perhaps one-third or more of the cards cut out of play—is hard work.

2. **CRAPS, pass/don't pass, come/don't come, with odds:** If blackjack playing conditions are subpar, that leaves craps as the game that

comes closest to giving the player an even break. The player who sticks to line bets with full double odds bucks only a six-tenths of 1 percent disadvantage. But the house edge jumps on other craps bets.

3. **BACCARAT; MINI-BACCARAT:** Strictly a guessing game—will the banker hand or player hand come closest to a total of 9?—baccarat has the relatively small house edge of 1.36 percent on bets on player and 1.17 percent on bets on banker. In the long run, bets on banker will win more often than they lose, but players must pay the house a 5 percent commission on winning bets on banker.

4. **CRAPS, place bets:** If you're going to venture away from pass/don't pass, come/don't come, stick to placing the 6 or 8. House edge here is only 1.5 percent. On the 5 or 9, the edge is 4 percent and on 4 or 10 it jumps to 6.67 percent. The player can bring that house advantage on 4 or 10 down to 4.76 percent by buying the numbers—paying the house a 5 percent commission in order to be paid true odds of 2-1 on winning bets on 4 or 10 rather than the 9-5 paid on place bets. Neither placing 5 or 9 nor buying 4 or 10 are among the best casino bets; they rank in a middle ground, along with playing roulette or the slot machines.

5. **BLACKJACK, average player:** When rating players for comps, many casinos assume about a 2 percent edge in blackjack. If the player plays a mimic-the-dealer strategy, always standing on 17 or above and hitting on 17 or below regardless of the dealer's up-card, or plays never-bust, always standing on 12 or more, the house advantage is closer to 5 percent. At 2 percent, this is still a better bet than most casino games; at 5 percent, it's no better than roulette. If you're going to play blackjack, learn basic strategy.

6. **VIDEO POKER:** In Nevada, where 9-6 Jacks or Better machines pay 99.5 percent with optimal play, video poker would be a strong contender for the top of the chart. But the house increases its edge by varying the payouts on the full house and flush. The full pay version pays 9-for-1 on a full house and 6-for-1 on a flush—hence, 9-6. The Illinois standards are 7-5 on quarter machines, with a payback of about 96 percent with optimal play, and 8-5 on dollars, for 97.3 percent. The average slot payout on the riverboats is a bit less than 93 percent, so the player who learns video poker strategy can do better than the typical slot player.

WORST BETS:

1. BIG SIX WHEEL: On a typical wheel, there are 54 slots, or on really big wheels a multiple of 54; 24 show $1 bills and pay even money if that's where the wheel stops; 15 show $2 and pay 2-1; seven show $5 and pay 5-1; four show $10 and pay 10-1; two show $20 and pay 20-1, and two different special symbols each pay 40-1. There's not a decent bet here. The house edge ranges from 11 percent on a bet on $1 to 24 percent on a bet on a special symbol.

2. CRAPS PROPOSITIONS: The one-roll bets on the craps layout are budget-killers. Look at these house advantages: any craps, 11.1 percent; 2 or 12, 13.9 percent; any 7, 16.67 percent. Avoid them; stick to the craps best bets listed above.

❧ 32 ❦
Image Aside, Baccarat
Is an Everyman's Game

In Las Vegas and Atlantic City, it's often the game of the "whales," the multimillionaires with huge credit lines, ready to bet tens of thousands of dollars—and more—per hand.

In the high-roller pits, it's the glamor game, where dealers wear tuxedos, and complimentary champagne buffets are laid out for the players.

And it's the game of privacy, where the private pits usually are secluded from foot traffic, and where security guards urge ordinary folk to keep moving in casinos where the tables are in view.

As a result, baccarat has a mystique, an unfamiliarity that can be intimidating to the average player. It draws the fewest customers of all the major table games in American casinos. In Illinois, the eight mini-baccarat and two baccarat tables in operation accounted for only $809,000 of the $26.4 million in casino gross receipts in August, 1994.

But baccarat (pronounced bah-cah-rah, though it's not unusual these days to hear back-a-rat) actually is the easiest of table games to play, and it offers even an inexperienced player some of the best odds in the casino.

In Illinois, the game usually is found on blackjack-sized mini-baccarat tables on the main casino floor rather than on big 15-player tables in private baccarat pits. The casino dealer deals all mini-baccarat hands, rather than pass the shoe among the players, as is traditional in high-roller baccarat games.

Regardless of the number of players, only two hands are dealt, one designated as the player hand, the other as banker. The game is a simple guessing game—which hand will come closest to a total of 9. Each card is worth face value—Ace is 1, deuce 2, etc. If totals reach 10 or more, the first digit is disregarded, so 10, Jack, Queen and King can be seen as having a value of 0. A 9 and a 6, totaling 15, would then have a value of 5.

After bets are placed—anyone can bet on either player, banker or a tie—player and banker are each dealt two cards. After that, taking a third card or standing on the first two is done according to a set of rules—there are no options.

The player hand is completed first. If the first two cards total 8 or 9, it is called a natural, and the player gets no more cards. Player also stands on totals of 6 or 7, and draws on all others.

Banker stands on 7, 8 or 9 and draws on 0, 1 or 2, but other hands depend on the value of the player's third card, in accordance with the standard rules available to players at all baccarat tables. Banker hits 3 unless player's third card is an 8; hits 4 unless player's third card is 1, 8, 9 or 10; hits 5 only if player's third card is 4, 5, 6 or 7, and hits 6 only if player's third card is 6 or 7.

There are a couple things not usually listed in the rules, but in force nonetheless. If the player holds a hand of 0, 1, 2, 3, 4 or 5 and banker has a natural, banker wins without player getting another card. If player has 6, 7, 8 or 9 and therefore does not receive a third card, banker stands on 6 as well as 7, 8 and 9.

When all that's done, the hand that totals closer to 9 is the winner. If the hand is a tie, both banker and player bets push, a bet on tie wins.

Don't worry about memorizing any of this—it's standard, there are no options and the rules are available at the table. So are score pads—many players like to track who wins each hand, then bet with the streaks.

Stay away from the bet on ties. It's paid at 8-1, but carries a hefty 14.4 percent house edge.

Banker wins more frequently than player, but the house charges a 5 percent commission on winning banker bets. The bottom line is a 1.36 percent house edge on player bets, 1.17 percent on banker bets. The only places in the house with lower percentages are blackjack, if the player takes the time to learn basic strategy, and craps, if the player sticks to pass/don't pass and come/don't come bets with full odds.

In baccarat, there is no strategy to learn and the game moves nowhere near as fast as craps, making it a good place for a novice table games player to begin.

❧ 33 ❦
Caribbean Stud Poker
Drops Anchor at Area Ports

Sometimes, the most memorable jackpots are those not won.

And in the first few weeks (in October, 1994) that casinos have been licensed to deal Caribbean Stud Poker in Illinois, there already is a horror story.

"I had a man get a royal flush," said Sonji, a blackjack dealer at Harrah's Joliet who has added Caribbean Stud to her repertoire. "And he didn't play the progressive. AND I didn't have a qualifying hand."

That meant Sonji's customer didn't win the progressive jackpot, a separate $1 bet, for his 1-in-649,740 shot. And since the dealer's hand wasn't Ace-King or better—a qualifying hand—the house folded and there was no 100-1 payoff on his bet. All he won was his ante, an even-money payoff.

So it goes in Caribbean Stud, an easygoing table game designed to appeal to jackpot hunters in today's slot-happy market.

The game, which rose to popularity in the late 1980s in the Caribbean and on cruise ships, combines the easy familiarity of kitchen-table poker with a video poker-like pay table and a slot machine-like progressive jackpot. That makes it a potential favorite in the '90s, when the industry's explosive growth in slot and video poker play has overshadowed table games.

Caribbean Stud spread to Las Vegas in the early '90s and already is a staple in Mississippi casinos. In Illinois, the Hollywood in Aurora became the first to introduce the game on Oct. 12. Harrah's and the Empress quickly followed suit.

"We're pleased to be the first riverboat in Illinois to offer Caribbean Stud Poker," said Patt Medchill, senior vice president for casino operations and marketing at the Hollywood. "It's a variation on poker—players can touch the cards and win large progressive jackpots. Our customers' first experience has been very positive."

It's a relaxed, slow-paced game, dealt from a single deck and played at about two-thirds or less the speed of blackjack. I played for a little more than an hour aboard Harrah's Southern Star recently, and played 34 hands. That pace will pick up a little as both dealers and players get used to the new game.

Played at a blackjack-sized, seven-player table, Caribbean Stud gives each player three places to wager—the ante, the bet and a slot for a $1 bet on the progressive jackpot.

After all players have anted and the dealer has checked to see that everyone who wants to make a progressive wager has done so, everyone is dealt five cards, with one of the dealer's turned face up.

Players pick up their cards and decide whether the hand is worth a bet. If they like their cards, they place a bet of twice their ante in the bet box. If not, they fold and the house collects the ante.

The dealer then turns his remaining cards face up. If his hand is Ace-King or better, it is called a qualifying hand and the rest of the hand is played out. If not, the house folds. The antes are paid at even money, but the bets are not called, so those wagers are returned.

If the dealer has Ace-King or better, the dealer then turns player cards face up and compares hands. If the dealer wins, the player loses both ante and bet. But if the player wins, the ante paid at even money and the bet is paid according to the rank of the player's hand—even money for a pair or less, 2-1 for two pair, 3-1 for three of a kind, 4-1 for a straight, 5-1 for a flush, 7-1 for a full house, 20-1 for four of a kind, 50-1 for a straight flush and 100-1 for a royal flush.

Best strategy is to bet on any hand of a pair or better, and on hands of Ace-King that includes a card of the same value as the dealer's up-card. That is, if the dealer turns up a 6 and your hand is Ace-King-9-6-3, play the hand; if your hand is Ace-King-9-7-3, fold it.

The progressive jackpot pays off on flushes or better regardless of the outcome of the hand. Payoffs range from $50 for a flush to the full amount of the progressive jackpot, which resets at $10,000 in most locations, for a royal flush.

Elliot A. Frome and Ira D. Frome, in their booklet *Expert Strategy: Caribbean Stud Poker,* estimate the house edge at 5.6 percent. That leaves it not as good a percentage wager as blackjack for a basic strategy player or the best bets on the craps table, but about the same as roulette and a bit better than slot machines. The house edge on the separate progressive wager depends on the level of the progressive jackpot—the break-even point is in excess of $200,000.

For the strict percentage player trying to grind out a small profit, Caribbean Stud will not go to the top of the list. But the casual player can relax here, kick back and take a shot at the kind of jackpot that slot players dream about.

❧ 34 ❦

When Busting is Worth the Risk
(And Other Strategy Tips)

A shuffle through the Gaming mailbag:

DEAR JOHN: *I can't abide going bust! So to make me feel better (I never go bust), several years ago I started staying on 12 and above. I feel good about myself and win on almost half my sessions. Can you tell me, mathematically, if this is wise, or just plain stupid and/or vain?*

Also, what do you think of this betting strategy? I bet the same, except when I win. While winning, progressively I bet 1-2-3-5-8-8-10-10-10 units, etc. When I lose, I go back to 1 unit. Assuming that I lose more hands than I win, any winning streaks can put me into a total winning situation. (I do not count cards. I split and double down according to the book.)

– Jack Bright, Elmhurst

Answer: Blackjack players tend to have selective memories. A bust when we hit 12 against a dealer's 2 sticks with us—never mind that more than twice as often, we don't bust.

In the long run, a never-bust strategy will do some damage to your bankroll. Playing basic strategy in a six-deck game in which the dealer stands on all 17s, pairs may be resplit and doubling after splits is permitted can leave you facing a house edge of just four-tenths of 1 percent. The never-bust player faces about a 5 percent house edge—12 times the basic strategy player's disadvantage.

Let's take a hit/stand decision that seems to trouble many players: a 16, with the dealer showing a 7. Now, 16 is just a bad hand, and you hit against a dealer's 2 through 6 in order to cut your losses.

If you stand on the 16 against a 7, you will lose all hands in which the dealer's down card is a 10, Jack, Queen, King or Ace for a total of 17 or 18. That's about 38 percent of all hands. In another 23 percent, the dealer's down card will be 2, 3 or 4 for a total of 9, 10 or 11, leaving the house in excellent position for a one-card draw for a total of 17 or better. And even if the down card is a 5 through 9, the house still can draw again.

The result is that the house will make 17 or better nearly 80 percent of the time when starting with a 7—and if you stand on 16, you lose every one of those hands. The percentages increase when dealer starts with 8 through Ace.

You're better off taking your own 38 percent chance to improve the 16 without busting than to concede the hand more than 80 percent of the time. So it is with any hand from 12 to 16 against a dealer's 7 or better. In the long run, your best play is to hit.

As for your betting progression, it can produce spectacular results when you hit a streak of several wins in a row. I've played a similar system, started with $100 at a $5 minimum table and won more than $300 in 45 minutes.

However, when you get a choppy deck in which most winning hands are followed by losses, you're worse off with a progression than betting a flat total on each hand. Let's say your betting unit is $5; you win your first bet, increase to two units, or $10, and lose. You've lost $5 over the two hands, whereas you'd be even had you been betting a flat $5 a hand.

Mathematically, the betting progression makes no difference over the long run. It can be fun to play and can lead to some big wins from time to time, but has no impact on the house edge over time.

DEAR JOHN: *A question concerning the video poker machines. If you put 25 cents in a regular draw poker (Jacks or Better) machine and get four Aces, you win 25 coins. If you play 25 cents in a Bonus Poker machine you win 80 coins for four Aces. Because you win more money on the bonus machine, is it harder to make that four Aces or any other four of a kind? Will that four of a kind come up more frequently on a regular machine?*

— Elaine Procento, Hoffman Estates

Answer: The hit frequency is the same on Bonus Poker as on a regular Jacks or Better machine. Cards are dealt from a randomly shuffled 52-card deck. The casino usually makes up the difference made by bigger payouts on four of a kinds by lowering the payouts on full houses; at the new Grand Victoria in Elgin, for example, regular Jacks or Better pays 7-for-1 on a full house, but Bonus Poker pays 6-for-1.

Typically, Bonus Poker Machines pay the normal 25-for-1 on four 5s through Kings, but raise it to 50-for-1 on 2s, 3s and 4s and 80-for-1 on Aces. Harrah's Joliet recently introduced Double Bonus Poker at the 50-cent and $1 levels. These machines not only pay 50-for-1 on four 5s through Kings, 80-for-1 on four 2s, 3s and 4s and 160-for-1 on four Aces, but also have a progressive jackpot on the royal flush. For a player who knows optimal strategy, the rate of four-of-a-kind hands actually increases slightly on Double Bonus Poker. The payback on four Aces is so big that the percentages actually call for the player to break up a pat full house with three Aces in order to take a shot at drawing the fourth Ace.

❧ 35 ❧

In Single-Deck Blackjack, It's Back to the Basics

Until the card-counting revolution came, blackjack was a single-deck game.

Through the 1950s, most casinos—which in the United States existed legally only in Nevada—played with a single deck, dealt from the hand. All player cards were dealt face down, and players were allowed to pick up their cards.

Usually a single card would be buried off the top of the deck. That card frequently would be shown to the players, and the rest of the deck would be dealt out.

When Dr. Edwin Thorp published *Beat the Dealer* in 1962, everything changed. Thorp's card counting guide was every casino executive's worst nightmare—a system that worked. A handful of players made big bucks and the casinos feared for their lives until a string of counter measures was developed.

First and foremost was simply barring anyone suspected of counting cards from playing. Card counting never has been held as illegal in any state, but in Nevada the courts have ruled that the casinos are private clubs and may enforce their own rules. In most newer gaming jurisdictions, counters cannot be barred.

Other changes have made today's game tough enough for all but the most skilled and dedicated counters that a casino rarely has to bar a player. Most games are multiple-deck, with up to eight decks shuffled together. Not all the cards are dealt out anymore; usually about one-third are cut out of play, and out of a counter's view.

To some blackjack old-timers, today's game seems a little sterile. All player cards are dealt face up in a multiple-deck game, and players are not permitted to touch the cards.

But every once in a while, particularly in Nevada, you can find the game dealt very nearly in the old way—single-deck, cards face down, players may handle the cards.

The trade-offs are that usually in modern single-deck games the dealer usually hits soft 17, a bad rule for the player; doubling down after splitting pairs usually is not permitted, and half the deck usually is cut out of play.

If you're sitting at a crowded single-deck table, you'll find only one hand dealt before a shuffle. That leaves no edge for a card-counter.

Sometimes a player will be lucky enough to find a game in which the dealer stands on all 17s and doubling after splits is permitted. The Frontier in Las Vegas dealt such a game through most of 1992 and '93; Circus Circus picked it up in '94, and shortly after it dropped the game in '95, the Riviera opened a few tables offering what used to be regarded as standard "Las Vegas Strip rules."

Half the deck still is cut out of play, so this is no card-counters' dream. But with that set of rules, a basic strategy player actually has an edge of one-tenth of one percent over the house, without counting cards.

However, single-deck does require some adjustments to the basic strategy for multiple-deck games presented here several months ago.

Here are where the games differ (player totals in boldface):

Hard 11: When the dealer shows an Ace in a multiple-deck game, it's best just to hit. In a single-deck game, double down against all dealer up-cards.

Hard 9: The difference comes when the dealer shows a 2. In multiple-deck, you hit; in single-deck, double down.

Hard 8: In the single-deck game, double down against 5 or 6, instead of hitting as in multiple-deck games.

Ace, 8: Good as that 19 looks, double down when the dealer shows a 6 in a single-deck game. When more decks are used, stand.

Ace, 7: Against an Ace, stand in single-deck blackjack, hit in multiple-deck. An exception: If you are playing in a casino in which the dealer hits soft 17, hit Ace, 7 vs. Ace in both single- and multiple-deck games.

Ace, 6: Double against a 2 in single-deck, hit in multiple-deck.

Ace, 3; Ace, 2: In the single-deck game, double these against 4, 5 or 6 instead of just against 5 and 6, as in the multiple-deck game.

2, 2: If doubling after splits is permitted, split against 2 through 7 regardless of the number of decks. If not, split against 3 through 7 in single-deck, 4 through 7 in multiple-deck.

3, 3: If doubling after splits is permitted, split against 2-8 in single-deck, 2-7 in multiple-deck. If not, split against 4-7 regardless of the number of decks.

4, 4: Never split if doubling after splits is not permitted. If it is, split against 4-6 in single-deck, 5-6 in multiple-deck.

6, 6: If doubling after splits is permitted, split against 2-7 in single-deck, 2-6 in multiple. If not, split against 2-6 single-deck, 3-6 multiple-deck.

7, 7: If doubling after splits is permitted, split against 2-8 single-deck, 2-7 multiple-deck. Split against 2-7 in doubling after splits is not permitted. Also, hit against a 10 in multiple-deck games, but stand in single-deck.

❧ 36 ❧

Games Expert's Message:
Tune In to Video Poker

Lenny Frome can't help but wonder at choices players make in newer gaming markets.

"What's wrong with people in the Midwest?" the Las Vegas-based Frome asked recently. "We send them our best machines, and they won't play them. I hear in Missouri they want to take 80 percent of video poker machines off the riverboats and put in slot machines."

Frome is the nation's leading expert on video poker, and his mission is to spread the word that with a little time spent on learning proper strategy, players will find that they receive a higher payback percentage and more frequent hits on video poker than on reel slots.

The author of several books on video poker, including *Video Poker: America's National Game of Chance* and *Winning Strategies for Video Poker*, Frome's latest effort to spread the word to the masses of slot players is a videotape, "Winning at Video Poker" (send inquiries to Lenny Frome, 5025 S. Eastern (16), Las Vegas, NV, 89119).

The tape is geared to what has become the basic game in the Midwest and South: 7-5 Jacks or Better.

"We built it around 7-5 machines, not only because that's what's available, but because you can use the same strategy for Bonus Poker and for 8-5 Jacks or Better, and 9-6 Jacks or Better is only a little different," said Frome, who worked in the aerospace industry for 30 years before becoming video poker's No. 1 guru.

In Las Vegas, 9-6 Jacks or Better, where a full house pays 9-for-1 and a flush pays 6-for-1, is regarded as a full pay machine. If you find a casino in which the Jacks or Better machines pay 8 on a full house and 5 on a flush (an 8-5 machine), most of the time you can walk next door or across the street and find the higher pay table.

Nevada customers, more attuned to the fine points of gaming than those in newer jurisdictions, are accustomed to looking for the best pay-offs. And video poker has become their game of choice. In Nevada casinos that cater to locals, 50 percent or more of machines usually are video poker.

That's not the case in newer jurisdictions—only 10 percent to 20 percent of machines are video poker. That's partly because of a perception that they are difficult to play and partly because the top jackpot—usually $1,000 for a royal flush with five coins played on a quarter machine, $4,000 on a $1 machine—does not reach the lifestyle-changing proportions a big reel slot jackpot sometimes yields.

However, strategy is easy to learn—nowhere near as complex as black-jack basic strategy, for example. And what those jackpots lack in size is more than made up in frequency. About 40 percent of all hands are winners, at least to the extent of returning your bet, on a Jacks or Better machine. Frome says even a 7-5 machine yields a 96.1 percent return with five coins in when played properly, much better than the average 93 percent return of all slot machines in Illinois.

"Even when played as badly as possible, by someone with no idea of how to play, these machines will return 89, 90 percent," said Frome. "But people still play these 88 percent reel slots."

Like reel slots, video poker machines are driven by a random number generator. But unlike reel slots, video poker is required to be dealt from a randomly shuffled 52-card deck, meaning all possible combinations and the frequency with which they will come up can be calculated.

Frome has done the homework, run it through his computer and come up with an estimated value for every possible play in video poker. That has led him to rank in order 34 hands worth playing. On any hand worse than No. 34—a three-card straight flush with both missing cards on the inside—all five cards should be discarded.

The video charts the playable hands and on those that are close calls explains why a particular play is made. For example, if you are dealt 8 of clubs, 8 of diamonds, 7 of diamonds, 9 of diamonds and 10 of hearts, there are three reasonable plays to choose from—hold the pair of 8s, hold the three card straight flush (7, 8, 9 of diamonds) or a four card straight, discarding one of the 8s. The video explains why the best play is to hold the pair of 8s, and therefore why a low pair ranks ahead of a four-card straight and a three-card straight flush on the list of playable hands.

For the player who has been intimidated by video poker or has been playing with no set strategy, "Winning at Video Poker" is an outstanding introduction to the hows and whys of the game. And for the more advanced player, the video accompanied by Frome's books makes a winning combination.

❧ 37 ❧
In Video Poker, It's Not
Just Luck of the Draw

Many casino old-timers still refer to "poker slots" when talking about video poker.

Like reel slots, video poker machines are governed by a random number generator that determines what combinations come up. And in the eyes of some, the "poker slots" are just trumped-up slot machines.

What makes video poker different is the requirement by state gaming boards that cards be dealt from a randomly shuffled 52-card deck—or, in the case of Joker Poker, a 53-card deck.

That means the frequency with which each combination will turn up can be determined mathematically. Odds can be calculated, and an optimal playing strategy can be devised.

Unlike reel slots, on which a player cannot tell the payback percentage by just looking at the machine, in video poker all the variables are known. The math has been done by experts such as Lenny Frome, who presents the findings in his books *Video Poker: America's National Game of Chance* and *Winning Strategies for Video Poker*, and mathematician Stanford Wong, whose computer program, "Stanford Wong Video Poker," is a terrific learning tool.

Strategies vary according to the type of machine and the pay table involved. The basic game is Jacks or Better, with a pair of Jacks, Queens, Kings or Aces returning the player's bet, the lowest return on the machine. Casinos usually change the payback percentage on Jacks or Better by changing the payout on the full house and flush. If the full house pays 9-

for-1 and the flush 6-for-1, you're playing a 9-6 machine, regarded as full pay in Las Vegas, gaining ground in Atlantic City and rare in the rest of the country. With optimal play, it returns an average of 99.8 percent.

More common outside Nevada and New Jersey are 8-5 (97.3 percent) and 7-5 (96.1 percent) machines. The strategy that follows can be used on either machine.

The following strategy ranks pre-draw hands in order. If your hand fits two categories, draw according to which hand ranks higher on the list:

1. Royal flush.

2. Straight flush.

3. Four of a kind.

4. Four-card royal flush. Not only does this give you a chance at the big payout, if your four-card royal is King-high, there is a chance at a 9-through-King straight flush, chances at other straights and flushes, and chances at high pairs.

5. Full house.

6. Flush.

7. 3 of a kind.

8. Straight.

9. Four-card straight flush, open on both ends. This hand—for example, 4-through-7 of spades—does not have the big bonus payout of the royal flush, and it doesn't have the high pair possibilities. But there are possible straights and flushes in addition to straight flushes. Break up a high pair to keep a four-card straight flush.

10. Two pair.

11. Four-card inside straight flush; for example, 4, 5, 7 and 8 of spades. There is only one card that completes this straight flush—the 6 of spades—whereas the open-ended version listed at No. 9 can be completed by either the 3 or the 8.

12. Pair of Jacks or better.

That brings us to the lowest-ranking winning hand. We'll pick up next week with a more difficult task—determining which hands are not winners before the draw but are playable.

AUTHOR'S NOTE: Since this was published in November, 1994, better-paying video poker machines have started to spread across the country. Full-pay 9-6 machines are common in Mississippi and are on some casino floors in parts of the Midwest. Some more complicated games, such as 10-7 Double Bonus Poker, with an average payback of more than 100 percent to the expert, also have hit the Midwest. Of course, very few casino-goers play at expert level; the house still makes money on these games.

❧ 38 ❧
Video Poker Games Pit
Man Against Machine

Until voters approved games of chance in November, Missouri divided casino games into two categories: Games of chance, such as roulette and reel slot machines, were out; games of skill, which in Missouri meant blackjack, poker, craps and video poker, were in.

That meant video poker held a special place in Missouri as the anointed player vs. machine game of skill. No dealers or other players to worry about; just play the electronic cards.

And video poker does combine skill with chance. It's not as pure a game of skill as live poker, where knowing your opponents and knowing yourself can be as important as the cards that are dealt.

There are no bluffs against the machine. The player merely tries to draw a hand that pays according to a table displayed on the glass, most commonly a pair of Jacks or better in this computerized version of five-card draw poker.

The skill comes in deciding which cards to hold and which to discard after the initial deal.

Keep in mind that when theoretical payback percentages are given in video poker, they are for optimal play. And optimal play includes not only making the best draw/discard decisions, but also playing the maximum number of coins.

Because of the big bonus for a royal flush with five coins in, the payback percentage is higher with the full amount played.

Video poker expert Lenny Frome has estimated that a royal flush should come up about once every 40,000 hands with optimal play. That may not seem worth worrying about, but look at what it does to the payback percentage.

If the machine is returning 96 percent with optimal play, that means that in 40,000 hands, with 200,000 coins played for maximum return, it is returning 192,000 coins. By prorating the payoffs for all hands but the royal, and assigning a 250-coin return for the royal on each of coins 1 through 4, we see that the average return is 37,850 coins, or 94.6 percent, on each of the first four coins.

But the fifth coin, with the big bonus, nets another 3,000 coins for the royal flush, bringing the total average return on the fifth coin to 40,600 coins every 40,000 hands, or 101.5 percent.

Last week we detailed the 12 highest ranking pre-draw hands for Jacks or Better video poker. This is a middle-of-the road strategy, usable on any common Jacks or Better machine, though there are expert variations for any given pay table. Following is a guide to the remainder of playable hands. If a pre-draw hand fits more than one category, keep the portion of the hand that ranks higher on the list, discard the rest.

Possibly the most important thing to note on this list is how high a low pair ranks. If you save a high card in hopes of getting a pair of Jacks or better, you will get more frequent payoffs, but you will hit more higher paying hands by saving the low pair.

Also, if you've played much live poker, you probably know never to draw to an inside straight. However, in video poker there are two exceptions—four high cards from Jack on up, and a four-card inside straight with at least three high cards—Ace, King, Jack, 10, for example.

Picking up from last week's list, here are the remainder of the playable hands in Jacks or Better video poker:

13. Three-card royal flush.

14. Four-card flush.

15. Four-card open-ended straight, three high cards.

16. Low pair.

17. Four-card open straight, one or two high cards.

18. Three-card straight flush, with two high cards.

19. Three-card open straight flush, one high card.

20. Four-card open straight, no high cards.

21. Three-card double inside straight flush, two high cards. (Double inside means both missing cards are on the inside. For example, 4-7-8 is missing 5 and 6, so it's "double inside"; 4-5-7 needs a 6 but could use either a 3 or an 8, so it's just "inside."

22. Three-card inside straight flush, one high card.

23. Three-card open straight flush, no high cards.

24. Four-card inside straight, four high cards.

25. Two-card royal, if the cards are King-Queen, King-Jack or Queen-Jack.

26. Two-card royal, Ace-King, Ace-Queen or Ace-Jack.

27. Three unsuited high cards, no Ace.

28. Four-card inside straight with three high cards.

29. Three-card double inside straight flush, no high cards.

30. Two high cards.

31. Three-card inside straight flush, no high cards.

32. Two-card royal, includes a 10, but no Ace.

33. One high card.

34. Three-card double inside straight flush, no high cards.

If your hand fits none of these categories, discard all five cards.

AUTHOR'S NOTE: A few readers expressed minor confusion when the preceding two columns appeared in November and December of 1994. What if your hand contains both a low pair and a four-card straight, I was asked. The answer is that you should check to see which hand appears higher on the list; if your hand is 9-9-Jack-Queen-King, for example, you have a low pair, listed at No. 16, and a four-card inside straight with three high cards, listed at No. 28 and three unsuited high cards, No. 27. Go with the higher ranking: Hold the low pair, break up the possible straight and discard the three high cards.

One reader also asked what you do with cards not part of the description. The column indicates that you hold two pair; do you hold the fifth card too? Of course, you must discard the fifth card and draw for a chance at a full house.

❦ 39 ❦
Looking for a Mantra
To Make the Slots Pay

A shuffle through the Gaming mailbag:

DEAR JOHN: *I have several questions.*

1. Does the casino have control over the slot machine for it to pay off? I notice when my player's card is in, I don't hit jackpots as much but when I take the card out, I do.

2. I heard it took three hours to pay off a $25,000 jackpot because they had to check the machine all out before they paid. Could that be true?

3. How are jackpots paid out? Do you have to pull so many times? Do you have to put in so much money to warm the machine up before it starts paying out?

4. How can you tell when a machine is ready to hit? Does the machine have to make a certain sound, click or jerk before it pays out? Does a certain symbol (a cherry, 7s, etc.) have to appear in a certain position, which will let you know that a jackpot is about to pay out?

5. Do you have to have a lot of points to win?

6. Do player's card points accumulate from Day 1 or just for that session?

– Joyce L. Harris, Gary

Answer: 1. The mechanism for tracking slot club points is separate from the random number generator that governs winning combinations and makes no difference as to whether you win or lose. If you have been winning more without your card, it is entirely by coincidence. Slot club players are among the casino's best customers, the ones who keep coming back time and time again. The casino is not likely to slight its best customers and risk losing them.

2. It normally takes 15 minutes, perhaps half an hour on a busy weekend night, to pay off a large jackpot. The combination on the reels does have to be checked against the computer record of the pull, but that doesn't normally take anywhere close to three hours.

Only if there is reason to suspect an irregularity would paying off a jackpot take so long.

3. Jackpots hit entirely at random—or as close to random as a person can program the random number generator to be. You're as likely to hit on your first pull as on your 10,000th.

4. The machine gives no signal that it is ready to hit. You cannot tell by looking or listening to a machine whether a winning combination will come up.

5. You don't need any points to win. I know of one woman who hit for $5,000 on the first pull she ever took on a slot machine. Of course, I know of many more people who have played for years without ever winning more than a few hundred dollars.

6. Slot club points accumulate every time you play. On systems that tell players how many points they have, they can see points they accumulated a year ago, if they haven't cashed them in, on the computer readout. Some clubs don't show the player point totals, but all track total play, along with frequency of play, in determining benefits.

DEAR JOHN: *In your column on Caribbean Stud, you mentioned that if the dealer up card is a 6 and my hand has Ace-King-9-6-3, I should play the hand; if my hand is Ace-King-9-7-3 I should fold it. I must be missing something because I thought the Ace-King-9-7-3 is a better hand. Should it be the opposite?*

– Darnell Allen, no address.

Answer: You're missing something. You play the first hand because the 6 matches the dealer up card. That shifts the odds on the dealer having a pair that would beat your Ace-King just enough to make the hand playable. The second hand, though higher ranking in a poker game, does not have a card to match the dealer up card and therefore has less chance of winning in Caribbean Stud. The object is to beat the dealer, and sometimes that means playing a hand that you would fold against a different up card.

❦ 40 ❦
Casinos Always Odds-On Favorites, Despite Systems

Gamblers believe in luck. They believe lightning will strike, that their time will come for the big hit, regardless of how improbable.

And all too often, gamblers believe in systems.

Casinos believe in mathematics.

Nearly every casino game—blackjack being the notable exception—carries a fixed mathematical edge. No matter how narrow that edge—and in craps the edge on a pass/don't pass bet with double odds is only six-tenths of one percent—the result over time is inevitable. The casino will grind out its profit.

But many players believe that a combination of bets—hedging that bet on red with a bet on the second 12-number column in roulette or guarding against the possibility of a pass-line bet losing on the come-out roll by placing a one-roll bet on any craps, for example—creates a synergy that will enable them to overcome the odds.

In a game with fixed mathematical odds, no hedging of bets can change the percentages. The notable successful casino gambling system—card counting in blackjack—takes advantage of constantly changing odds. In blackjack, the odds are not fixed; they change as cards are dealt. That's because the composition of the deck yet to be played changes. Each card dealt affects the probabilities for succeeding hands. When a high percentage of remaining cards are Aces and 10-value cards, the odds swing in the player's favor. The card counter raises his bets.

But craps and roulette offer no similar situation. Each roll or spin is an independent trial, each facing the same odds as the previous roll or spin. The dice have no memory, the experts like to say. It doesn't matter if a 7 has just been rolled. The odds of it coming up on the next trial still are 1 in 6. The percentages never change.

Nevertheless, the belief that somewhere out there is a system the casinos can't stop has led some unscrupulous businessmen to a can't-miss system of their own—selling systems to the unwary. People who find their names on mailing lists of gamblers sometimes receive offers that detail how to beat craps, roulette, blackjack, even slot machines. Unlimited riches are offered, all for only $35, or $100, or $1,000.

It's easy to devise a system that wins more often than it loses. The trick is to devise a system that wins more money than it loses, for the major flaw in most systems is that a single loss wipes out the profits painstakingly built with a series of smaller wins.

Let's take a simple example in craps. A place bet on 6, in which the bettor wages that a 6 will be rolled before the next 7, has five ways to win and six ways to lose, because there a six ways to roll 7 with two dice and five ways to roll six. Likewise, there are five ways to win and six ways to lose a place bet on 8.

But what if we combine the two wagers, making place bets on both 6 and 8? Now there are 10 ways to win and only six ways to lose. In the long run, the bettor will win an average of 10 of every 16 rolls that lead to a decision. Yes, the bettor will win 62.5 percent of the time.

However, that's not as rosy a situation as it looks on the surface. Place bets on 6 and 8 pay 7-6, so let's assume that each bet is for $6. The 10 wins in an average 16 decisions will yield $70. But on the losing rolls, our systems bettor is losing both on the 6 and on the 8, for $12 per loss. There are six losses in our example for a total of $72. So our bettor, while winning 62.5 percent of the time, is losing money.

Most betting systems involve more complex combinations and hedging of wagers, but the principle is the same. Mathematicians have been telling us as long as there have been games of chance that the house percentage will hold up in the long run, and no system of interactive wagers and money management can overcome a mathematical edge.

For those who devise such systems, if they really believe they've done the impossible and found a flaw that has escaped generations of mathematicians, there are a couple logical steps. First, rather than selling systems, go to the tables and win enough money to live comfortably the rest of your days. Second, submit your work to the Nobel committee.

On the other hand, for those tempted to buy such systems, a word of caution: Buying the system is unlikely to prove nearly as expensive as using it.

❧ 41 ❧
Bettors' Systems Often Just Organized Way to Go Broke

Systems players are nothing if not persistent.

There are betting systems that have been around for decades or more, all thoroughly discredited to the point that nearly every basic gambling text carries a warning never to use them.

But these methods live on. In the last several months, I have received letters on each of the following systems from readers who say either they have tried these systems or have friends who have recommended them.

Any one of these systems can be profitable in the short term. Then again, disaster could strike at any time, including the first time a player uses any of them.

A word of caution before describing these persistent systems: Never use any method that requires you to increase your bets when you are losing. That is one way gamblers get in serious trouble, as losses get bigger and bigger in a bad streak. The time to increase bets is when you are winning. Don't fall into the following traps.

Martingale: In this system, the bettor doubles his wager after each loss. If the first bet in a sequence is $5 and the bettor wins, he takes the $5 profit and starts a new sequence. If the bettor loses, his next wager is $10, then $20 and so on until he wins.

After any winning wager, the bettor shows a profit equal to his first bet—$5 in our example. If he loses at $5, $10 and $20 for a total of $35 in losses, but wins at $40, he has a $5 profit, then starts a new sequence with a $5 bet.

If the bettor had an infinite amount of money and the casino would accept infinitely large wagers, this system would work every time.

However, Martingale numbers get very large very quickly. We've gone to the fourth level—$40—with a $5 starting point. Next come bets of $80, $160, $320, $640, $1,280.

Our bettor starts running into table limits rapidly. Some casinos limit maximum wagers at $5 minimum tables to as little as $300, meaning that after losing a sixth consecutive bet, a wager large enough to recoup losses no longer is accepted. Other casinos accept $500, even $2,000 bets at $5 tables. Even so, wagering $1,280 after eight consecutive losses for a chance to show a $5 profit sounds like nerve-wracking situation.

Martingale players argue that the chances of so many losses in a row are remote. But in a dead-even game, a player will lose six bets in a row to start running up against table limits an average of once every 64 trials. And casino games are not even. In roulette, for example, the chances of winning an even-money bet are not 50 percent, they're 47.37 percent, and that six-loss streak will show up about once every 47 trials. That gives our bettor 46 wins at $5 each for $230, but the one losing streak in an average sample, with bets of $5, $10, $20, $40, $80 and $160 will total $315. And there's no telling when that one big loss will come.

Grand Martingale: This is even worse. Not content with squeezing out a one-unit profit with each win, the Grand Martingale player adds an extra unit in addition to doubling up after each loss. After a $5 loss, the next bet is $15—$10 for doubling the original bet, $5 for adding an extra unit. Next in the sequence is $35, then $75, $155, $315. At a $300 limit table, a $5 Grand Martingale player runs up against the table maximum after losing five bets, instead of six as in a regular Martingale. It's a quick way to go broke.

Cancellation: Bets don't increase as rapidly as in the Martingale or Grand Martingale, but in the end this system popular with roulette players is just a slower way to lose money. The player starts by writing a series of numbers, and the total is his win goal for the sequence.

It's most common for a cancellation series to start with three numbers, but it can start with as few as one. Let's just start with a three-number cancellation—1, 1, 1. The win goal for the sequence is three units, or, for a $5 bettor, $15. Each bet will be the sum of the numbers on each end. Here, the starting point is two units, $10. If the bet wins, the bettor crosses off, or cancels, the number on each end, then bets the sum of the new end numbers. In this case, if the first bet won, the second bet would be the remaining number, one unit, or $5.

If the first bet loses, the player writes the number of units bet at the end of the sequence. Here he's left with a new sequence of 1, 1, 1, 2. The next bet becomes the sum of the new end numbers—three units, or $15. When all numbers have been crossed off, the player has reached his win goal.

The bets do not quickly reach the astronomical range of the Martingale. However, neither does a single winning bet end the sequence. With a perfectly ordinary sequence such as a win, two losses, a win, three losses, a win, two losses, the sequence grows and the losses mount.

❧ 42 ❧

House Holds Onto Edge
Against Progression Betting

Streaks happen.

Sometimes, the ball will drop into a red number six or eight times in a row at the roulette wheel. Or a craps shooter will make pass after pass for a half hour or more. Or a blackjack player will win several hands in a row.

That has led gambling authors from Lyle Stuart in his 1978 book *Casino Gambling for the Winner* to Donald Dahl in 1993's *Progression Blackjack* to counsel betting with the streaks, increasing bets while winning, then bringing bets back down after losses.

And if the gambler knew when streaks were beginning or ending, that would all be very profitable. But no one knows there has been a streak until it is over, and then it's too late to jump on. If red has come up five times in a row, all you know for certain is that there has been a streak of five spins; that does not change the house's 5.26 percent edge on the next spin.

All that leaves "bet with the streaks" as the casino gambling equivalent of the old stock market adage, "Buy low, sell high." If only we could identify the highs and lows before they happen.

Nevertheless, many players enjoy using progressive wagering systems. In the long run, these systems cannot overcome or even diminish the house's mathematical advantage, but they can on occasion lead to large wins. And unlike systems in which the player increases wagers after losses, these progressions will not lead to quick bankruptcy in a losing streak.

Because increased bets are funded by money won from the house—don't call it "their money"; once you've won it, it's yours to do with as you please—the player has a chance to make larger bets and win larger amounts without digging deeper into his original bankroll.

Let's say a roulette player is betting a flat $5 on red on each spin. If red has come up six times in a row, the player wins a total of $30.

But what if the same player uses a conservative betting progression, starting with $5 bets, increasing to $10 after two consecutive wins, then to $15 after two $10 wins? (The progression moves after two winning bets at each level so the player never risks being behind for any sequence starting with a win. If he wins two $5 bets, then loses at $10; he's even. If the progression moved ahead after each win, one win at $5 and a loss at $10 would bring a net $5 loss.)

With that progression, after six consecutive red numbers, the player will have won $60—twice as much as the flat bettor.

After one loss, the player brings his wager back to the original level. So if after six wins, our red bettor loses $20 on spin No. 7, he locks up $40 in profits and starts a new sequence with a $5 bet.

The logic of progressions moved Dahl to subtitle his book *Exposing the Card Counting Myth and Getting an Edge in 21*, and to tout progression as the way to beat blackjack in the era of multiple deck shoes in which one-third or more of the cards may be cut out of play, making life difficult for a card-counter. Card-counters also require larger initial bankrolls than progression players, because counters increase their bets as the count becomes favorable, regardless of how much they've won or lost to that point. Progression players increase only when winning.

That logic is not without fault, however.

If a progression player encounters a perfectly ordinary sequence of win two bets, lose two, he finds himself behind for the sequence. Taking our $5 bettor, two winning $5 bets, followed by a $10 loss, then a $5 loss, results in a net loss of $5. A flat $5 bettor would be even, with two $5 wins and two $5 losses.

Second, by definition, a progression player always loses the largest bet in a sequence. Bets are increased until there is a loss, then brought back down. A progression player would win his largest bet only if he'd decided he'd won enough and walked away before a loss to end the sequence. Card counters, on the other hand, reduce bets as the composition of the deck remaining to be played turns less favorable. So counters can win their largest bets.

Finally, counters identify situations in which there is a large concentration of 10-value cards and Aces remaining to be played, favoring the player, and bet accordingly. Progression players increase their bets after a couple wins and decrease after losses regardless of the composition of the deck remaining to be played. So sometimes they miss favorable situations, and sometimes they increase their bets into negative situations.

In the long run, a progression player, with some large wins but more frequent losses, bucks the same percentages and will have about the same overall success as the flat bettor, and will not do as well as a skilled blackjack card counter.

The bottom line: Progressions can be fun, but don't expect miracles.

❧ 43 ❧

Hedging Bet on a Roll
Might Get You Rolled

A shuffle through the Gaming mailbag:

DEAR JOHN: *If you have $5 on the pass line, is it worth it to put $1 on any craps on the comeout roll to kind of hedge your bet?*

— John B., Riverside

Answer: No. The house percentages on proposition bets are just too high to make them worthwhile in any circumstances. In the case of any craps, there are two ways to roll 3 with two dice, one way to roll 2 and one way to roll 12, for a total of four craps rolls. With 36 possible two-dice rolls, that means an average of one of every nine rolls will be any craps, making the true odds 8-1. But the house pays only 7-1 on the any craps bet, giving the house an advantage of 11.1 percent.

Let's take a series of 36 comeout rolls in which every possible combination comes up once. Your $5 pass line wager will win on the six 7s and two 11s, lose the four times any craps shows up, and a point number will be established the other 24 rolls. That's the same, regardless of whether you've also played any craps.

But on the one-roll any craps bet, you will have won four times, for $28 in winnings, and lost your $1 bet 32 times for a net loss of $4. So you're out an extra $4.

You'll find similar results for any other proposition bet commonly used as a hedge—after a point is established; for example, some players like to bet any 7 despite its 16.67 percent house edge. The enormous house percentages make such hedge bets just a faster way to lose money.

Dear John: *I am unclear on the term "soft 17" as opposed to 17. Could you explain this term to me?*

– Jesse James, Chicago

Answer: In blackjack, a soft 17 is a hand that includes an Ace or Aces and could be counted either as 7 or 17. The most common soft 17 is Ace-6, but Ace-2-2-2, or Ace-Ace-5, or a number of other hands that total 17 but could be used as 7 are soft 17s. The same definition applies whenever we speak of "soft" totals. Ace-3, or Ace-Ace-2, or Ace-Ace-Ace-Ace, are soft 14s, for example.

DEAR JOHN: *Your Nov. 18 column (column number 36 in this book) states that Missouri wants to take 80 percent of video poker machines off the riverboats and put in slot machines. I hope that the Illinois riverboats don't plan on eliminating poker machines also. The reason I go is to play the poker machines.*

– Elaine Procento, Hoffman Estates

Answer: You need not worry about video poker disappearing. If anything, you'll see more of it as players get more experienced. That's what has happened in the older gaming markets of Nevada and New Jersey, where player demand has led to ever increasing video poker options.

Missouri is a special case, because reel slots were illegal until voters OKd games of chance in November. Casinos had been operating with video poker, deemed to be a game of skill, but no reel slots. Now reel slots are being moved onto the boats.

❦ 44 ❦

Tale of Two New Games: One Success, One Struggle

Success breeds imitation. And in the world of casino table games, Caribbean Stud Poker has been a success.

Enough players have taken to the twist on five-card stud poker that casino operators have been encouraged to try other reworkings of established games.

On a recent trip to Las Vegas, I had a chance to observe two games that are new variations on old themes. One appears destined to make its way into casinos across the country. The other seemed to be getting so little play that it may struggle for survival, even in Las Vegas.

Here's how they stack up:

LET IT RIDE: Like Caribbean Stud, this is a variation on five-card stud poker. They share several of the same strengths—Americans' easy familiarity with poker hands, a video poker-like pay table and customer satisfaction with being allowed to handle the cards as opposed to just using hand signals, as in multiple-deck blackjack games.

It does not offer a big, slot machine-type progressive jackpot as Caribbean Stud does, although in Nevada there is a tournament option, whereby players who hit a big hand with a $1 side bet in play are invited back periodically for a multimillion dollar tournament. The house edge in Let It Ride is about 2.5 to 3 percent, according to Lenny Frome, the video poker expert who also does the math for many game developers for their gaming board presentations.

Like video poker, there is no dealer hand to beat in Let It Ride. All bets are paid according to a table, with a pair of 10s being the lowest-ranking winning hand.

Play starts with each player making bets in each of three circles in front of him. If the player does not like his cards, he may pull back the first or second bets.

The dealer, using a single 52-card deck, gives each player three cards, face down. Two more cards are placed face down in front of the dealer. The player makes a poker hand out of his own three cards plus the two in front of the dealer.

After all cards are dealt, each player picks up his three cards. Players then have the option to pull back the first bet by scratching the table with the cards or to let the bet ride by placing the cards face down next to the chips. The dealer then turns over the first of the two cards shared by all hands, and players have the option to pull back the second bet. The third bet must stand.

Finally, the dealer turns up the second shared card, then turns up player cards in turn to settle all bets.

If a player does not have at least a pair of 10s, the dealer collects the remaining bet or bets. If the player has a pair of 10s or better, the remaining bet or bets are paid at even money; other returns are 2-1 on two pair; 3-1 on three of a kind; 5-1 on a straight; 8-1 on a flush; 11-1 on a full house; 50-1 on four of a kind; 200-1 on a straight flush, and 1,000-1 on a royal flush.

Let It Ride appeared to be getting heavy play in Las Vegas—more, even, than Caribbean Stud. Expect this game to spread.

QUICK-DRAW BACCARAT: The future may not be quite so bright for this simplified version of baccarat. Baccarat is not as familiar to most Americans as five-card stud—the full-scale, ceremonial version always has been reserved for the high-rollers and mini-baccarat has been less than an overwhelming success.

Developers had hoped that by streamlining the arcane hit/stand rules that even many regular baccarat players never committed to memory and by eliminating the commission paid to the house on winning bets on the banker hand, they could make the game more accessible to the public.

Like baccarat, a player hand and a banker hand are dealt, and the customer may bet on either hand. The hand that totals closer to 9 wins. The streamlined rules call for either hand to stand on 6, 7, 8 or 9, and either hand to draw to 0 through 5.

Either hand is as likely to win as the other, and there are no commissions involved. The house gets its edge by declaring any winning hand totaling 2 a push—there is no payoff. That gives the house an edge of 1.1 percent on either bet.

On a percentage basis, Quick-Draw is one of the best bets in the house—only good blackjack players, craps players who stick to the best bets on the table and video poker players who choose the best machines and use proper strategy do better.

But all hit/stand decisions are according to the rules, so there are no player decisions to make. And the game moves very fast—with the dealer hitting according to set rules and dealing only two hands regardless of the number of customers at the table, this game moves at craps-like speed. Figure to play twice as many hands per hour as at a busy blackjack table.

A visit to Bally's on a crowded evening found only one customer at Quick-Draw. That's not enough evidence to pronounce the game a failure, but don't expect to see it in most gaming areas anytime soon.

AUTHOR'S NOTE: In October, 1995, seven months after this column appeared, I had a discussion with the inventor of Quick-Draw Baccarat at the World Gaming Expo in Las Vegas. "I know who you are," he said, eyeing my name badge. "You didn't like my game." It's really not that I don't like Quick-Draw. As stated in the column, it's an easy game with a low house edge. I just thought—and still think—that the average non-baccarat player might find the unfamiliarity and speed of the game intimidating.

❧ 45 ❧

Some Casino Standbys
Still Resist the Video Age

The video revolution and the computer age changed the face of the casino industry long ago—but not without some failures.

The most notable flop has been the inability of video slot machines to attract customers. Video poker has been enormously successful, though it has had a slower start in the Midwest than in other gaming areas. And video keno, though not as widespread a success as poker, has carved out a niche in the market.

But there has been no niche for reel slots on a video screen. When video slots were introduced in Nevada, slot players stayed away in droves, making clear they wanted to see actual reels spinning, not a computerized simulation.

"Reno was the first to come out with video reel machines, and if people came within 10 feet of them they felt they were too close," remembers Keenan Wright, slot director at the Empress in Joliet. "They hated 'em."

"It all goes back to the perception that it's not a game, it's a computer, and people don't want to play against a computer. There's a bias there in that people feel a computer game is able to be manipulated. It's something the industry has tried very hard to overcome."

As it happens, slots with physical reels also are computer driven, and there's nothing a manufacturer can do with the programming for a video slot that it can't also do to a reel slot. Still, customer resistance has been strong.

That doesn't mean slot manufacturers are ready to give up on putting their games on video screens. In fact, casino-goers should be ready for a new wave of video games, this time with a twist: Manufacturers are using touch-screen technology to put several games on the same machine—something that could be especially appealing to riverboat casinos with their space limitations.

Harrah's Joliet slot director Don Wren is interested in trying the machines both on Northern Star and Southern Star, "if it ever gets approved (by the Illinois Gaming Board). We had planned on putting five on each boat." But the Gaming Board has not yet licensed the machines for use in Illinois, so Wren is still waiting.

Multiple-game machines manufactured by Bally's already are on the floor in several Las Vegas casinos. The machine displays a video menu, customized to the casino's specifications, of available reel slot, poker and blackjack games. The customer touches the on-screen icon for the desired game, which then comes onto the full screen. Just as on regular reel slots or video poker machines, there are buttons on the console to spin the reels or draw the cards.

"It should appeal to the younger market, people who are computer literate, used to video and the computer thinking process," says Wren.

Video poker expert Lenny Frome says that in larger Las Vegas casinos, with no shortage of poker or reel slot options, video blackjack has been getting the most play on the multi-game consoles—surprising in that video blackjack never has attracted much of a following.

"I certainly wouldn't worry about that happening here," says Wren. "Video blackjack has been the worst performing game on the boats. We only have one left on Northern Star. The rest we changed out for poker."

Wright said colleagues in Las Vegas had told him of the video blackjack play.

"One guy told me he had just taken out a bank of video blackjack and replaced it with touch-screen machines," says Wright. "Every time he walks past, people are playing video blackjack. Amazing. It just shows you're never quite certain what's going to happen in this business."

If the public accepts the machines—particularly the reel options—it could lead to the biggest change in casino technology since the introduction of video poker in the late 1970s.

"Overall the video product available is not changing dramatically," says Wren. "There's not a lot of innovation. People are tired of purchasing and playing the same thing over and over."

But, says Wright, a new age of innovation may be near.

"Ultimately, probably everyone tends to agree, touch screen games will take us into the future," says Wright. "The technology has the potential to show us new things we haven't even dreamed of. More options—that's the excitement of the gaming industry. It'll take a while, but the future of gaming could be very exciting."

And when the public is ready for the new technology, Wren hopes to be one step ahead.

"We'll have what the customers want," he says. "Hopefully, we'll have it first."

AUTHOR'S NOTE: By late 1995, Empress had become the first Chicago area casino to add Bally's Game Maker multiple-game machines with video poker, blackjack, keno and reel slots. From all reports, they've received heavy play. I have no breakdown yet, however, on which games the customers play most.

❧ 46 ❧

At the Blackjack Table,
Forget Other Players

People sometimes have odd ideas about the game of blackjack—usually about what other players should do.

A recent week brought a letter, a phone call and a conversation with a co-worker, all dealing with the same situation—what is the player's duty to the rest of the table?

The answer will not please some people who grimace every time another player takes the card that would have busted the dealer's hand, or who fret over the competence of every player at the table: It makes no difference in the long run what the other players do.

"There's what we call selectivity of memory at work," says Anthony Curtis, publisher of the monthly Las Vegas Advisor newsletter and a former professional gambler. "They remember all the times a player made an error and it cost them, but they don't remember, or don't even notice, the times that another player making an error caused the dealer to bust.

"Studies have been done with mathematics and computer analysis to see if a poor player affects a perfect basic strategy player, with a table full of basic strategy players and one poor player or a couple poor players, and the results are that the basic strategy player is unaffected by the play of others at the table."

The letter writer, the caller and the co-worker all brought up similar situations, involving players' decisions on what to do with a 12 when the dealer's up-card is a deuce. The writer and caller both were sitting at third base, the seat all the way to the players' left and the last position to make a hit/stand decision before the dealer. Both decided to hit the 12, both drew 10s to bust—10s that would have busted the dealer—and both drew nasty remarks from other players about taking the dealer's bust card.

As it happens, both players made the right play. They'll win more often by hitting the 12 against a 2. Sometimes other players will be helped, sometimes others will be hurt, sometimes they'll be unaffected. In the long run, it will all balance out.

Curtis' advice for the player who doesn't like the abuse heaped on this third baseman? "No. 1, don't play there," he says. "Don't put up with that garbage. This guy made a good play (by hitting the 12)—in fact, a great play—and took heat for it.

"Some people think they can control play better by sitting at third base and not let a poor player sit there. But to a basic strategy player, it makes no difference if the third baseman is a poor player or not. So if it makes no difference, you might as well not sit there."

The co-worker's situation was slightly different. Not sitting at third base, he hit a 12 and drew a 7. Because he hit, the dealer, with a deuce up and a 10 down, drew another 10 to bust. Another player congratulated him on the play.

Later, the player who had offered congratulations stood on a 12 vs. a 2. My colleague asked why, and the player said it was because the player to his left was going to need a hit, and he didn't want to take her card. When my colleague responded that he thought that was odd, that hitting was the right play, the man and woman responded that sometimes you have to do it for the table, and if he didn't want to play that way, they were leaving. And they did.

But there is no real reason to worry about the play of others. Others' decisions will help you as often as they hurt you. The greatest harm that can come from others' decisions is harm you do to yourself—letting that factor interfere with your concentration to the point where it affects your playing or betting decisions. If you find that happening, the best thing to do is to find another table.

Besides, sometimes the biggest heat goes to the best players.

"A really experienced player who is counting cards might sometimes hit a 16 against a 2 and wind up taking the dealer's bust card," Curtis says. "You should hear the other players then. And here he's just made this great high-level play. It's all a little bizarre."

❧ 47 ❧

In World of Gimmicks,
Leave Laptop at Home

A shuffle through the Gaming mailbag:

DEAR JOHN: *I have read in your past columns about gimmicks and systems to beat the house. I believe you said the casinos welcome them all. Last year I attended a seminar, and the gentleman claims he has a hand-held computer that will tell him what number to bet. He claims he can't lose on any spin of the roulette wheel. His theory is he can break even but never lose (strong statement). He also claims he can win $1,100 an hour on a minimum of $5 bets. Now my question is, will any riverboat casino allow this kind of computer to bet on roulette? Last year he wanted to have the seminar in Atlantic City, if they would let him use the computer. The answer was a flat NO. What is your opinion?*

– Frank Ellioan, Waukegan

Answer: Whenever someone claims to have a foolproof gambling system, my advice is to keep your money in your pocket and walk swiftly in the other direction. The claim that any system, computer-aided or not, can guarantee instant profits with no risk of loss in roulette or any other game is outlandish.

In most gambling jurisdictions, use of computer gambling aids is illegal—it's not just the casinos that prevented this gentleman from using his system. But the reason for the computer ban has little to do with roulette. The late Ken Uston, whose *Million Dollar Blackjack* and *Uston on Blackjack* are classics, for a time used a hidden computer to determine optimal bet size and playing strategy at the blackjack table. He and his team made fabulous profits before laws were passed banning the computer. But blackjack, in which odds change constantly as cards are removed from the deck, is a far different story than roulette, in which the house has its 5.26 percent edge on every spin.

There is reason for casinos to fear use of a computer by roulette players, but not because of large, short-term player wins. It is possible for a player using a computer to track and analyze thousands of spins over a period of days, and occasionally find a biased wheel in which a few numbers show up more frequently than they should by random chance. With knowledge of that bias, the player could turn the odds in his favor. Even on a biased wheel, the player wouldn't win or break even on every spin, but would turn a profit over a longer period.

DEAR JOHN: *Last time I was in Las Vegas I started playing a game called pai-gow poker. I was wondering if there are plans to bring this game to the riverboats here?*

– Steven A. Bernstein, Chicago

Answer: You'll probably not see pai-gow poker on the riverboats in the near future. The problem with the game, from a casino operator's standpoint, is that it moves too slowly, that most hands end in pushes, leading to an average of only about 10 decisions per hour. The large resort casinos of Nevada can afford to use space to offer extra gaming options. On the riverboats, with their space limitations, operators would rather use the space for more profitable games.

In pai-gow poker, players and dealer (or banker—a player may act as banker in this game) each receive seven cards, which they then set into a five-card poker hand and a two-card hand. The five-card hand must outrank the two-card hand, or the player loses. If both player hands beat the dealer, the player wins; if both dealer hands beat the player, the house wins; if they split, the hand is a push and no money is exchanged. The house edge comes from two sources—the player pays a commission, usually 5 percent, on any winning hand, and if either the five-card or two-card hand ties the dealer, the dealer wins that portion. That happens most often on the two-card hand—if both player and dealer turn up Ace-10, for example, the dealer's two-card hand wins.

DEAR JOHN: *Why don't the riverboats have blackjack machines? Poker machines are all over the place, but since I prefer 21 and can't always find a $5 or $10 table open, I always enjoyed playing the machines instead. Is there a reason for the scarcity of them?*

— Ellen Wohl, Glenview

Answer: You apparently were one of the rare few to play blackjack machines—they just didn't receive enough play to justify their space on the floor. Don Wren, director of slot operations at Harrah's, says blackjack machines were the worst-performing machines on the boats. Most have been removed in favor of machines that get more play.

❧ 48 ❧
Proper Money Management
May Conserve Your Bankroll

Anyone who has played in a casino more than once has an idea of what he's going to do for the day each time he goes.

Maybe the plan is to head straight for the slot machines, or for the blackjack or craps table. Maybe it's to try something new this time—the slot player might be ready to give video poker or blackjack a go, or a roulette player might think Caribbean Stud looks interesting.

But too many players fail to plan how they intend to manage their money with anything like the detail they plan which games to play. And money management is every bit as important as choosing the games themselves.

Here are some do's and don'ts to help your bankroll survive a casino visit:

DO bring a gambling bankroll you can live with. Consider gambling an entertainment expense, and bring what you can comfortably spend on a day's entertainment. Sometimes you'll win, more often you'll lose a little, but there will be days that you'll find you're losing bets as fast as you can place them. When that happens, you don't want to be spending the grocery money or the mortgage payment. Don't gamble with money you can't afford to lose.

DON'T overbet your bankroll. If you've set $50 as the amount you can afford to gamble, don't bet $5 a spin at the roulette wheel or $5 a hand at Caribbean Stud or blackjack. Ten hands and you could be done for the day. You need to have a large enough bankroll to survive the inevitable swings in fortune. Otherwise, the first downturn can wipe you out, leaving no chance for a comeback. With $50, that limits you to quarter slot machines or video poker, unless you happen to be playing in an area with table minimums lower than $5.

DO set loss limits at each table or machine, and stick to them. If you buy in for $100 at a $5 blackjack table, you don't have to stay until the $100 is gone. Instead, try setting a loss limit of half your buy-in. In this instance, if you lose $50, leave the table. You can buy in at another table or change games or just take a walk. But it's important to know for yourself that you have the self-discipline to walk away from the table with money.

I like a system of floating win goals and loss limits. A reasonable win goal for a $100 buy-in is $20—or 20 percent of your buy-in. That doesn't mean you walk away from a table that has been good to you when you reach $120. Instead, you re-assess. Raise the loss limit to $60—half of $120—and raise the win goal to $145—$120 plus 20 percent, rounded to the nearest $5. Each time you reach the higher win goal, re-assess again.

If the cards stay hot and you find yourself ahead even more, put the original $100 back in your pocket, play only with the winnings and set a loss limit based on them. Do not give it all back.

DON'T raise your bets when losing in an attempt to recoup losses. Chasing losses is a good way to self-destruct. There is no evening-out factor or law of averages that applies in any term so short as a casino visit, or even a year's worth of casino visits for one player.

The odds remain the same on every roll of the dice or spin of the reels, regardless of how your luck has been the last couple hours. If your luck has been bad and your bankroll is running short, play more conservatively, decrease your bets or just quit betting. Save that last 10 bucks for lunch.

DO re-invest part—but not all—of your winnings. If you've had a good run on quarter slot machines and have won a couple hundred dollars going into the last 20 or 30 minutes of your stay, by all means, take $50 or $100 and try your hand at a $1 machine or at a table game. But first, put away your original investment plus at least half your winnings—not to be touched again, regardless of what happens at the higher level.

❧ 49 ❧
A Sure Bet: Answers
To Your Most-Asked Questions

More than 500 letters and faxes from readers have arrived in the year since the "Gaming" column first appeared in the Chicago *Sun-Times* on Feb. 18, 1994. (Note: This column originally appeared Feb. 17, 1995.)

Many of these have appeared in frequent periodic shuffles through the Gaming mailbag. Others have become column subjects.

A few questions are asked over and over—once a month or more. Here's a look at the questions readers ask most:

Question: *How do you become a dealer?*

Answer: For the most part, riverboats in the Chicago area hire dealers from the ranks of employees. Your best chance to become a dealer is to take another job in the operation—bartender, security guard, coat check person—and stick it out until you're eligible for the dealers school.

Question: *Can you send me information on how to play (craps, blackjack, roulette)?*

Answer: I have no pre-printed information to send out. To readers asking for how-to-play information, I've sent some book recommendations, and I'll be doing several columns with mini-reviews of books on several casino games. My own book, titled *Winning Tips for Casino Games*, is due for September publication by Signet Books.

Question: *How do slot machines work? Do you have to take so many pulls before it is due for a jackpot?*

Answer: Reel combinations on slot machines are as random as it is possible to program a computer to make them. Modern slot machines are governed by a microprocessor with a random number generator, and there is no discernable pattern to when winning combinations hit. You're as likely to hit on your first pull as on your 100th.

The odds of hitting any particular combination are the same on any given pull. If a machine's top jackpot is programmed to hit, on the average, once every 10,000 pulls, that percentage will hold up over hundreds of thousands or millions of pulls. But the odds against a player hitting that combination on any given pull are 9,999-to-1, whether it's the first pull or 10,000th.

Question: *I seem to win more when I play without my player's card. Is it worthwhile to join slot clubs? Which club is best?*

Answer: The magnetic reader that tracks your play at slot machines is a separate mechanism from the random number generator. It has nothing to do with whether you win or lose.

The cards are free, and complimentaries and perks make it worth joining the club at every casino you visit. Empress offers free admission to card holders, and Harrah's frequently comps admission to those who use its Gold Card. That puts the Joliet boats on an even keel with Hollywood and Grand Victoria, which do not charge admission fees.

Which is best depends on individual preferences. Harrah's, Hollywood and Grand Victoria allow slot players to see their point totals and choose their own comps. At Empress, players must ask an Empress Club representative for specific comps. For example, you might ask if you have enough points to get a credit voucher for the food court.

Table players must request specific comps at all four area operations. Harrah's, Hollywood and Empress rate table players at all levels—a $5 or $10 player won't get his lunch tab picked up every time, but if he plays frequently enough, he'll get it sometimes. At Grand Victoria, table ratings start at the $25 level.

Question: *Which boat do you like best?*

Answer: I try not to play favorites, and have recommended different boats to people looking for different things in a casino. People choose a casino for many different reasons—a non-smoking table games player might prefer Empress II; someone who likes a party atmosphere might choose Harrah's Southern Star; a discerning video poker player might like the 25-cent 7-5 Bonus Poker machines at Hollywood, and someone who likes a big casino feel might prefer Grand Victoria.

For myself, the first two things I want to know about a casino are the rules and playing conditions in blackjack, and the video poker pay tables. These are the games in which the player's skill makes the most difference, as well as being the games in which there is the widest variation in playing conditions. Empress currently offers the best blackjack conditions, followed by Harrah's, Hollywood and Grand Victoria. In video poker, Harrah's is the leader, followed by Hollywood, Empress and Grand Victoria.

❧ 50 ❧
To Learn the Games,
You Go Buy the Book

On a recent visit to Las Vegas, I dropped into the offices of the Las Vegas Advisor, an outstanding monthly newsletter that happens to have more subscribers in Chicago than anywhere else in the country.

In the course of conversation, publisher Anthony Curtis asked, "How did you learn?"—a natural enough question of a Midwesterner who did not grow up in the shadow of the Las Vegas Strip or any other casino area.

The answer is that it was partly experience, with occasional trips to Las Vegas—there is no substitute for actually playing the games in a casino environment. But just as important was the time between trips spent reading about casino games, odds and strategies. It's easy enough to tell by looking around at decisions made by other players that basic blackjack strategy and an understanding of the odds at craps do not come naturally.

Hundreds of gambling books are available, ranging from the basics for beginners to advanced theories and strategies for experts. This week, we'll look at some general guides, covering most casino games. These are pretty easily available—I've seen every one of the books listed below in local book chains in the last year. Later, when we look at books on specific games, I'll review a few that aren't so easy to find. For hard-to-find gambling books there are a few good sources, all offering free catalogs: the Gamblers Book Club (800-522-1777), the World's Greatest Gambling Catalog (800-345-7027) and the Gamblers Edge (4344 S. Archer, Suite 143, Chicago, IL 60632-9927; write for catalog).

Many general gambling guides still on the shelves show their age—blackjack, slots and video poker have changed a great deal since the Edwin Silberstang and Len Miller books listed below were first published in 1980 and '83, respectively. And video poker didn't even exist when John Scarne's book came out in 1961. Still, as introductions to casino games, these books serve a purpose. Here's a look at four of the most easily available guides:

The Winner's Guide to Casino Gambling, by **Edwin Silberstang** (**Signet Books**): A very entertaining read with loads of personal anecdotes. On games that haven't changed much in the last 10 or 15 years—craps, roulette, baccarat, keno—Silberstang is very solid. Blackjack is a bit of a problem, as it is in many general gaming guides, in that it describes a game that no longer exists. Many of the anecdotes—such as a cat-and-mouse game with the dealer using a tip as incentive for the dealer to deal deeper into the deck—are specific to a single-deck game in which the dealer has an option of whether to keep dealing or reshuffle, and no longer apply to today's game. Likewise, he describes slot machine odds in terms of the number of symbols on each reel and the number of possible combinations. This no longer applies in the days of microprocessors and random number generators. **Rating: ★★★**

Casino Magazine's Play Smart and Win, by **Victor H. Royer** (**Fireside Books**): Royer is the slot machine columnist for Casino Magazine, and his 1994 book is an attempt to reflect the way games are actually played today. Naturally, he's strongest on slots and video poker. The book does require a careful read, though—Royer frequently sets up an oversimplified example, then goes back in subsequent paragraphs to give a better explanation. His explanations of rules and strategies are easy to understand, and novices will find this a useful book. Some of his strategies are at odds with other experts—for example, he suggests betting on craps and 11, a poor percentage move, when making a pass-line bet on the comeout roll in craps. **Rating: ★★½**

The Gambling Times Guide to Casino Games, by **Len Miller** (**Lyle Stuart**): It's down to the raw basics here—162 pages, and that includes games not commonly found in casinos, such as backgammon and gin rummy. Still, Miller packs the dozen or so pages he's able to devote to each game with solid information. Be alert for his craps strategy—he packs it into little more than a page under the headings "Best Betting" and "Get

Smart," then spends 3 ½ pages on the less-recommended method of covering the numbers with place bets. The blackjack chapter is a simple description of the rules, followed by a basic strategy chart with no explanation. So it goes here—a good basic guide of how to play, but for elaborate explanations of strategies, you'll need to look elsewhere. **Rating: ★★½**

Scarne's New Complete Guide to Gambling, by John Scarne (Fireside Books): This big, green, 871-page monster by the late John Scarne seems to be on the shelf of any store that stocks books on gambling. And if we could turn the clock back 20 years, I'd give it an unqualified recommendation. It's a fascinating read for anyone interested in the history and development of games of chance. Unfortunately, it lists copyright dates of 1961 and 1974, is out of date on slots and has nothing on video poker. It holds up well on table games, and gives more complete explanations of odds and probabilities than most newer books. **Rating: ★★ (current utility); ★★★★ (gaming history).**

❧ 51 ❧
What Percent of Gambling
Dollars Do Casinos Keep?

A shuffle through the Gaming mailbag:

DEAR JOHN: *Could you publish the percentage of gambling dollars that is returned to the gamblers vs. what is retained by the casinos in Illinois as opposed to the percentage in Nevada? I heard that in Illinois 17 percent is returned and 83 percent retained. In Nevada, the numbers were reversed, with 83 percent returned to the gambler and 17 percent retained by the casinos.*

– Steve Hamaden, Wheaton

Answer: Casinos need winners to spread the word almost as much as they need losers to generate profits, and any casino that kept 83 percent of the money played soon would find business drying up. The games in Illinois are basically the same as in Nevada. The blackjack's a little tougher here, and pass-line bettors in craps can back pass-line bets with only double odds as opposed to up to 10 times odds in Nevada, but roulette, mini-baccarat and Caribbean Stud are exactly the same games in both states.

In December, the latest figures available from the Illinois Gaming Board, casinos here retained 19.59 percent of table games buy-ins, a number that's right in line with Nevada figures. Broken down by individual operations, casino win percentages ranged from 17.12 percent at Harrah's to 26.74 percent at Casino Rock Island.

This is not the same figure as the house edge. The casino win percentage represents the percentage of all buy-ins retained by the casino after players are finished playing and replaying their money for the day. For example, on the average, a roulette player facing a 5.26 percent house edge would have about $95 left after playing $100 through once, then $90 after replaying the remainder, and so on. If he quits with $80 left, having lost $20, the casino win percentage is 20 percent.

Illinois lags slightly behind Nevada in slot machine payout percentages, but nothing like the reversal you suggest. In December, machines here paid back 93.55 percent of all money dropped in, ranging from 94.3 percent at Casino Queen in East St. Louis to 90.87 percent at Players in Metropolis. Payouts in Las Vegas average a little better than 94 percent on the Strip, a little better than 95 percent downtown.

The slot payout percentage is equivalent to the house edge—a machine that returns 93.55 percent carries a 6.45 percent house edge—and does not take into account the effect on your bankroll of replaying your returns.

DEAR JOHN: *On Feb. 17, your column states the Empress is offering the best blackjack conditions. Please explain why. I gamble at the Grand Victoria and would like to know what makes one boat better than the other in the game of blackjack.*

– Steve Schaffer, Franklin Park

Answer: The two major differences among blackjack games near Chicago are the number of decks in play and whether the dealer stands on all 17s or hits soft 17. The fewer decks, the better for the player. And it is better for the player if the dealer stands on all 17s.

Empress offers a six-deck game with a good set of rules that would be right at home on the Las Vegas Strip—not one of the best games, but not one of the worst, either. The dealer stands on all 17s, players may split any pair—including Aces—up to three times for a total of four hands, players may double down on any two cards and may double after splitting pairs.

Harrah's and Hollywood differ from Empress mainly in that they deal from eight-deck shoes. That adds a couple of hundredths of a percent to the house edge. In addition, Hollywood players may not resplit Aces. That leaves the house edge at 0.33 percent at Empress, 0.35 percent at Harrah's and 0.43 percent at Hollywood.

Until recently, Harrah's offered a six-deck game that was equivalent of Empress' game for a basic strategy player. The only thing that separated the two Joliet games was that Empress cut only about one deck out of play, while Harrah's cut about two decks. Now, however, Harrah's has switched to eight decks.

Grand Victoria uses six decks, but the dealer hits soft 17. That tacks roughly two-tenths of a percent onto the house edge against a basic strategy player, and takes Grand Victoria's overall edge against a basic strategy player to 0.62 percent. To play a game in which the dealer hits soft 17, I would want to see some powerful compensating rules. In Vegas, single- and double-deck games in which the dealer hits soft 17 are common, and the most playable six-deck game with this rule, at the Las Vegas Club, allows the player to double down after three cards in addition to the usual option after two, along with other liberal rules.

AUTHOR'S NOTE: By early 1996, Harrah's had converted most of its tables back to six decks, Hollywood mixed in some six-deck tables in its high-limit pit and added two-deck and four-deck games with rules that are tough on the player, and Empress had a few eight-deck tables to go with its six-deckers. Grand Victoria's game remained constant.

❧ 52 ❧
Electronic Keno Gives
Bettors Steady Action

Casino games do not always easily coexist in live and electronic versions.

Video blackjack has never built much of a following, while the live version is the most popular table game in U.S. casinos. Mechanical or video versions of roulette and craps have been tried, with little success. Video poker has become a casino staple, but it's so different from live poker that it might as well be considered a completely different game.

Then there's keno.

It can be played in a lounge, with players marking cards as they try to guess which numbered balls will be forced out of an air blower. Some would say the live version, most common in large, land-based casinos, is a game to savor; others find it mind-numbingly dull. Either way, the pace is slow, with fewer than 10 "races," as the games are called, per hour.

Though the game has its devotees, many players use live keno as a diversion, stopping to relax over a drink in the keno lounge, or playing a couple of races over a meal in the casino coffee shop, where keno runners pick up marked tickets and bets, and later return to pay off winners.

The electronic game—the only version available in Illinois—is anything but relaxed. A player who wants to use the same numbers over and over can get in as many trials as any slot player—hundreds per hour.

Still, they're basically the same game, derived from the Chinese Lottery. Early in keno's American history, each number was assigned the name of a racehorse. That led to the name "racehorse keno," and to each game being known as a "race." Horses' names were removed in the early

1950s in Nevada—then the only state where the game was legal—because of a new tax on off-track betting. With a tax in the picture, casino operators didn't want their game misconstrued as horse wagering.

Both versions start with 80 numbers. Twenty are drawn, either through the forced air blower in most live games or by a random number generator in the electronic version.

The player tries to guess which numbers will come up, though he doesn't necessarily try to guess all 20. He can mark a single number (a one-spot ticket), or anything up to all 20 numbers in live keno. Video keno usually limits the player to 10 spots. The more spots marked, the larger the payoff if the ticket hits.

There are partial payoffs if some of the player's numbers hit. Payoffs vary among casinos, but a player might find a four-spot ticket that for a $1 wager pays back $1 if two numbers hit, $5 if three numbers hit and $120 if all four are drawn, for example.

The one advantage that the live game has over the video game is flexibility. A single ticket can be marked as a straight ticket, way ticket, king ticket or combination ticket. On the straight ticket, a player marks the number of spots desired and makes a single bet. In our four-spot example, the player would mark his numbers, write "1/4" on the side of the ticket, and would be eligible for any four-spot payoff.

But the player also could draw one circle around two of the numbers and another around the other two. Then he could mark the ticket "2/2, 1/4," playing each of the circled two-number combinations as a two-spot, and all four numbers as a four-spot, essentially making three bets on the same card.

When a player circles a single number of the group he has marked, he is playing a king ticket. The single number is the king, and is used in all combinations. If he adds a fifth number to the example above and circles it, the player might mark "2/3, 1/5" meaning the king is used with each of the two-number combinations to form two three-spots, as well as with all other numbers to form a five-spot.

And the player can circle several groups of numbers and play combinations together. A two-number grouping can be combined with a three-number grouping and another of four numbers that reads "1/2 (the two-number set by itself), 1/3 (the three-number set), 1/4 (the four-number set), 1/5 (the two- and three-number sets), 1/6 (two- and four-number sets), 1/7 (three- and four-number sets), 1/9 (all three groups)." On this combination ticket, the player makes seven different bets.

Video keno doesn't have this flexibility—a straight ticket is the only kind you can play on the electronic version. But video keno has its own advantage—it pays better. A survey of live keno tickets in Nevada casinos last year found payback percentages from below 70 percent to near 80 percent.

Pay tables also vary on the video game, but they're competitive with other slot machines, usually around 90 percent at the quarter level.

As for strategy, there really isn't one. Play birthdays, anniversaries, lucky numbers. It really doesn't make any difference—provided the numbers really are random.

❧ 53 ❧
How Two Keno Players
Beat Impossible Odds

Regular readers of this column probably have seen the phrase "random number generator" more times than they care to count.

The random number generator determines the combinations that come up—winning or otherwise, on electronic gaming devices such as slot machines and video poker machines.

Combinations are as random as it is possible for a human to program a computer to generate. A slot player should not be able to detect any pattern of wins and losses.

But how close to random can a program designed by humans be? Recent events in keno have caught the attention of Lenny Frome, a longtime aerospace engineer who has become the nation's leading video poker expert.

The event that shook the keno world occurred early last year in Montreal at the Casino Montreal. The casino offers live keno, but instead of using numbered balls in a forced-air blower, Casino Montreal chooses winning numbers electronically with a random number generator.

Daniel Corriveau discovered a pattern in the numbers generated and used his knowledge to pick 19 of 20 numbers in three consecutive keno games.

What's more, according to the biweekly newsletter Gaming Today, he did it by using different number combinations in each game played, bucking all but impossible odds of 1 in 25,570,606,400,000,000,000,000,000,000,000,000,000,000. As Gaming Today, based in Las Vegas, put it, if a person played a million keno games every second, 24 hours a day, he would be expected to hit 19 of 20 numbers in three consecutive games just once every 3.156 quadrillion centuries.

After much wringing of hands, gnashing of teeth and investigation, Corriveau was paid his winnings of $600,000. The random number generator designers replaced the computer chip.

That prompted Frome to send along the following essay:

"Two recent events have involved people succeeding in winning at keno by virtue of their astute observations or their specialized knowledge. Both events involved the keno games' random number generators. The fact is that there is no such thing as a true random number generator; i.e., an electronic device that over the long term outputs an equal amount of every number in a way that is totally unpredictable. What we have are pseudo-random-number devices.

"In the first keno-busting case, a Canadian player (Corriveau) noticed that every morning the keno numbers were the same as the previous morning. The casino was mistakenly resetting the RNG to the same starting point by shutting off the equipment every night. The equipment didn't have the means to keep running continually, nor a 'seed generator' to start it up in a different place the next morning. The player won $600,000 in a couple of days of easy pickin's. (To throw authorities off the track, the player claimed he used a complicated model based on chaos theory to select his numbers.)

"In the second instance, a former employee of the Nevada Gaming Control Board allegedly used privileged information about the RNG and its seeding, along with a laptop computer, to figure out where the RNG was in its cycle. On 10 tickets, one came in for $100,000.

"Both incidents involve special circumstances, and neither should cast doubts in the minds of players about the integrity of the games as they apply to everyday play."

The special circumstances Frome points out are special indeed. The Nevada case involved inside information. And the Montreal case would never have happened in a 24-hour casino, where power to the random number generator is never shut down. At 24-hour casinos, the generators go on generating numbers all the time, whether in play or not. Any patterns would be extremely, if not impossibly, difficult to spot.

In addition to his astute observation, the key for Daniel Corriveau was that in keno, unlike other electronic games, winning numbers are generated in every game. For Corriveau, it was just a matter of marking and playing the numbers he knew were next.

❧ 54 ❧

U.S. Requires Casinos
To Report Big Players

A shuffle through the Gaming mailbag:

DEAR JOHN: *I would like to know the law on gambling. The casino told me I lost $10,000 when I lost only $9,000. I had $800 left and they told the dealer I could not play. They said they wanted my driver's license and Social Security numbers, and that I had to fill out a form. Also, I am curious as to why I have to double my bet if I play two hands.*

– Name withheld

Answer: The $10,000 limit you refer to is a federal anti-money-laundering regulation. It has nothing to do with how much you've won or lost, just how much cash has changed hands. It is the same regulation that applies to banks handling large cash transactions or to car dealers if a sale is made for cash. Any cash transactions totaling $10,000 or more in a 24-hour period must be reported. You can hit the limit without winning or losing a cent, as long as your buy-ins and cash-ins total $10,000 or more.

As for the requirement that you play twice the table minimum to play two hands at once, that's a common house rule at most casinos. They would rather take the chance that another player will make larger wagers on a open betting spot than allow one player making minimum bets to tie up two spots.

DEAR JOHN: *I need the definitive answer on when and what is reported to the IRS as it applies to gambling winnings. Somebody just came back* *from Vegas and said they won $1,600 on a slot machine and had to sign for it! Not that I'll ever have this problem, but it's something to ponder.*

– Sam Canzoneri, Chicago

Answer: Casinos are required to report to the IRS any slot machine hit of $1,200 or more or any keno winnings of $1,500 or more. In addition, tournaments are held to be contests, and winnings of $600 or more must be reported by the casino. I ran into this last rule a couple of years ago in Las Vegas when I won $1,000 in a slot tournament. Along with my winnings, paid in cash, I was given a form to fill out for the IRS.

Check out the payouts for top jackpots on slot machines, especially at the quarter level. You'll find a few that pay out $1,199—just $1 below the total at which the casino would be compelled to take identification of the customer and report the winnings to the IRS.

If you play in casinos with any frequency, it is a good idea to keep careful records of places and times you've played, amounts of buy-ins and amounts of cash-ins. All gambling winnings are taxable, but losses are deductible up to the amount of winnings. If you use a players card, most casinos can verify the dates you've played. Some will even give you a computer printout of your profit/loss statement on electronic games. They have no way of keeping a precise total of your wins and losses at the tables, but as long as you use your card, everything you put into and take out of a machine is tracked electronically.

DEAR JOHN: *You have printed the slot machine payoffs for the riverboat operations in Illinois. I do a lot of gambling on slots on the Indian reservations in Wisconsin. What are the payoffs at Ho-Chunk and Oneida? I want to gamble at the place with the best payoffs.*

– Joe Lovergine, Chicago

Answer: Unfortunately, payoff percentages at tribal casinos are not routinely released to the public as are the percentages in Illinois or most other states with legalized casino gambling. In Illinois, each casino reports to the Illinois Gaming Board, and the Gaming Board releases the statistics monthly. Tribal casinos report to the federal Indian Gaming Commission, which puts out no such regular statistical report. If Ho-Chunk or Oneida chooses to release the information to me, I'd be happy to run it.

DEAR JOHN: *I am curious how to handicap horses. I have been to many a casino that offers horse racing in its sports book operations. I love to see the horses run, although I am not an educated handicapper. Could you please do an article on how to handicap horses?*

— No name

Answer: I would not think of stepping on the turf of my old friend Dave Feldman, the Chicago *Sun-Times'* turf editor and handicapper. For handicapping advice, see Dave's column in the *Sun-Times* sports section.

❧ 55 ❧

Compulsive Gambler
Changes Her Luck

Nearly four years after making her last bet, Carol O'Hare still has to check herself.

"To this day, if you see me walk through a casino, I have my hands either in my pocket or I have something in my hands, even if I'm just holding my locket," she says as she grasps the pendant and chain about her neck. "I have to know what my limits are. There are some days I take a walk across the casino floor even if I don't have to, because I need that reality check."

A compulsive gambler with a problem that once was so deep that, she says, "I had nothing left to lose but my life," O'Hare today plays a role in helping others recognize, understand and confront compulsive gambling. As a consultant to Harrah's Responsible Gaming Program, she travels across the country to help develop and evaluate programs, and to tell her story to Harrah's managers and employees.

She tells of a four-year plunge that left her in a near-suicidal state before she finally found help. "Not that I keep statistics," she says, "but my last bet was made Jan. 31, 1991. If I had my almanac with me I could tell you how many days."

An Illinois native who moved before casino gambling was legalized, O'Hare showed no signs of a gambling compulsion here. In Nevada, it was another story.

"When I got to Vegas I started casino gambling, primarily video poker," she says. "As it progressed and I grew more dependent, my behavior patterns changed. I found I wasn't comfortable in casinos anymore. I started playing in bars, laundromats, grocery stores. If you could gamble there, I did it.

"I was having financial difficulties, but I was able to convince myself that they weren't that great. Compulsive gamblers have a tremendous capacity for lying to ourselves. I told myself I enjoyed it, I had a good feeling. It took a while before I realized that good feeling didn't exist anymore. I was gambling to stop the pain, mostly from gambling the day before."

Once the realization came that gambling had become a means of numbing herself to the reality of a ruined life, she found she couldn't stop. Compulsive gamblers have to hit bottom, she says, often committing acts of desperation, before they recognize that they need help.

When she came to grips with suicidal feelings, O'Hare finally sought help.

"I went through a 12-step program and the most shocking piece of information I found at that first meeting is that I was not the only person in Las Vegas living that kind of lunacy.

"These were perfectly normal people; they weren't all smoking cigars or standing in the shadows or showing tattoos. I walked in and thought, 'I don't get it.' These were normal, average people. Every person in that room had already been through what I was going through. I was not unique. It was a shock. I told my story, and they all smiled and nodded. They'd already been through it.

"And of course as I told my story it hit me that if they can be like this, calm, laughing, there must be a way to change this."

Many compulsive gamblers, says O'Hare, think they're alone in their problem. They don't realize help is there. And that's where projects like the Responsible Gaming Program come in. The program is divided into Project 21, to raise awareness of the consequences of gambling among those not of legal age, and Operation Bet Smart, which provides information on the problem to employees, guests and the casino industry.

In Joliet, Harrah's is sponsoring a Project 21 poster and essay contest at Joliet Central High School, Joliet Junior College, Lewis University and the College of St. Francis. New nationwide is a help line (800-522-4700) being launched by the National Council on Problem and Compulsive Gambling. Harrah's is funding development, staff training and first-year expenses, while AT&T is donating funds toward equipment costs and setup.

The key, says O'Hare, is information, right down to the phone number for the Illinois Council on Problem and Compulsive Gambling (800-

GAMBLING, or 800-426-2546) that appears on Harrah's advertisements and promotional materials. No one can force a compulsive gambler to get help, she says, but the information on how to get help must be available.

"This is not about money," she says, "it's about people. I try to help (people at her talks) understand that the effects of compulsive gambling extend beyond anything you may see on the casino floor. It has a real impact on the family and on the community.

"Just like any other addiction, you don't stop gambling forever. You stop today. When you wake up tomorrow, you make the choice again.

"The reason I've been fortunate enough not to make a bet since then is that I really believe that for me, I don't know if I have another recovery left in me."

❧ 56 ❧
Books That Help You
Get a Handle on Slots

Slot machines are the simplest casino games to play—just drop in your money, pull the handle and wait for a result.

They're also the most misunderstood games in the house. Some slot players believe they should keep playing a machine that has not been paying out, because it is "due." Others see that same machine as "cold," one to avoid until it starts paying out. Some think the casinos can change the payout percentage with the flip of a switch, or make the machine pay a jackpot at the push of a button.

Players hold all these misconceptions because they do not understand the basics of how a slot machine works. This column addresses all these ideas from time to time—"Gaming" receives more letters about slot machines than about anything else.

There also are several books on the market for people who have more than a casual interest in the one-armed bandits. Here are three that are widely available. If you can't find them in your local bookstore, ask the bookstore to order from the publisher, or try the Gamblers Book Club, (800) 522-1777.

Break the One-Armed Bandits, by **Frank Scoblete** (**Bonus Books, Chicago**): This 1994 publication is built around an interview with "Mr. Handle," a casino executive who did not give his real name. Mr. Handle describes the psychology of placing higher- and lower-paying machines in the casino, and gives some general guidelines on how to find the higher-paying slots. The guidelines are easier to practice in larger land-based casinos than on the small riverboats of Illinois and Iowa, where the slots usually are arranged in rows for space purposes. Larger casinos have room for the slot crosswalks and circular slot carousels described by Scoblete.

Don't expect to instantly spot a 99-percent payback machine in a sea of 92-percenters. But slot players will find this a fun guide to what areas of a casino to seek out, and what areas to avoid.

Slot Machine Mania, **by Dwight and Louise Crevelt (Gollehon Press, Grand Rapids, Mich.):** First copyrighted in 1988, *Slot Machine Mania* is strong on explaining how machines work and on debunking common misconceptions.

With sections on jackpots and big winners, superstitions, even cheating and safeguards, it's written in a breezy, entertaining style. There's the student from Arizona who dreamed of being a millionaire by age 35, and who made it at 23 by hitting five 7s on a Maximus Millions slot machine at Caesars Palace. And there's the casino owner who disguised herself as a change girl to go on the lookout for dishonest players and employees.

John Patrick's Slots, **by John Patrick (Citadel Press, New York):** John Patrick's works are not for everyone. He believes in trends, streaks and systems, systems, systems, all of which draw raised eyebrows from most other experts.

Still, Patrick is strong on detailing bankroll requirements for playing the slots, and he gives much solid money management advice. Unlike blackjack or video poker, slot machines leave the player no decisions that can affect the outcome of play. Playing the slots is a money management game, and those who do not manage wisely will lose quickly and often.

❧ 57 ❦
Double Bonus Poker
Offers Top Rewards

There is a frequent correspondent to "Gaming" named Howard Stern—no, not *that* guy—who checks in whenever a percentage or strategy listing goes awry.

His passion appears to be video poker. His notes are accompanied by detailed strategies for different pay tables, compiled by plugging the pay variations into the Stanford Wong Video Poker program.

Stern's latest missive couldn't have come at a better time. Just two days before it arrived, I'd cruised on Empress I and found a bank of 25-cent Double Bonus Poker machines. And stunningly, the pay table was the full-pay Las Vegas version, returning an average of 100.2 percent over the long run with optimal play.

With this one bank of machines, Empress leaps into the race for best video poker in the Chicago area, an area dominated recently by Harrah's. For $1 players who take the time to learn only one video poker strategy, the 9-6 Jacks or Better machines on Harrah's Southern Star are still best in the area, returning an average of 99.5 percent with optimal play. Also, the 50-cent Loose Deuces Wild progressives and the $1 Double Bonus Poker progressives aboard Southern Star exceed 99 percent at the rollover value of 4,000 coins for five played for a royal flush. One percent of all coins played are added to the royal jackpot, a fast-moving progression that frequently pushes the payoff high enough that both machines often exceed 100 percent payback for those who use optimal strategy.

Double Bonus Poker varies from regular Jacks or Better on two pair, straight, flush, full house and four-of-a-kind paybacks. Instead of the standard 2-for-1 payback on two pair, Double Bonus Poker pays back just 1-for-1. That's a huge cut, because players using an optimal Jacks or Better strategy will find that two pair comes up about once per eight hands.

However, Double Bonus Poker more than makes up that difference in the full-pay version by paying 10-for-1 on a full house, 7-for-1 on a flush and 5-for-1 on a straight. On a full-pay Jacks or Better machine, those figures are 9-for-1, 6-for-1 and 4-for-1, and the most common quarter machines reduce that further to 7-for-1, 5-for-1, 4-for-1.

On four of a kind, Double Bonus hikes the standard 25-for-1 payback to 50-for-1 at most denominations, 80-for-1 on four 2s, 3s or 4s, and 160-for-1 for four Aces.

A single four of a kind can keep the player going for a long time. And the 160-for-1 payback on four Aces—$200 with the full five coins played on a quarter machine—is an attractive secondary jackpot to the big royal flush payout.

Payback percentages vary with changes in the payback on the full house and flush. The Harrah's Southern Star $1 machines reduce the full house payback to 9-for-1, and on Harrah's Northern Star the 25-cent machines reduce the full house to 9-for-1 and the flush to 6-for-1.

Playing Double Bonus Poker at optimal level does require some strategy variations from regular Jacks or Better. We'll discuss them next week.

⟿ 58 ⟾
Strategy for Best Payoff
In Double Bonus Poker

The best video poker machines offer players some of the best odds in the casino—much better than other electronic gaming devices such as slot machines, better than craps, even better than blackjack for all but the most skilled card-counters.

However, few players get what they should out of video poker. Last week, "Gaming" described the new full-pay Double Bonus Poker machines aboard Empress, with 100.2 percent paybacks for optimal play. (That percentage is under dispute, by the way. Machines that pay out more than 100 percent are illegal in Illinois, and Roger Shields of the Illinois Gaming Board says Double Bonus Poker yielded less than 100 percent over millions of plays, in computer tests using an optimal strategy. Video poker expert Lenny Frome prefers to put the payout at "very close to 100 percent," but he says the Gaming Board must have been using a less-than-optimal strategy.)

Reader Howard Stern, who derived a playing strategy for the machines from Stanford Wong's Video Poker computer program, says he recently saw a computer printout of the performance of Double Bonus Poker at Colorado casinos, and that the public actually was getting 3.5 percent less than the potential payback.

This is not entirely a bad thing—if every video poker player used optimal strategy, casinos would be unable to offer such high-percentage machines, just as if every blackjack player used perfect basic strategy, the casinos would have to downgrade the house rules to ensure their profits.

But that doesn't mean you have to give any extra edge to the casino. Following is the strategy Stern sent in. Keep in mind that payback percentages listed are for optimal play over the very long term—in one session or even several sessions, you'll sometimes find yourself losing so rapidly you'll have to break off the session.

In the table that follows, higher ranking options are listed first. For example, when your first five cards give you four cards to a royal flush, No. 4 on the list, hold those four and draw one card even if it means breaking up a flush (No. 7), straight (No. 9) or high pair (Aces at No. 12; Kings, Queens or Jacks at No. 16). However, a straight flush (No. 3) outranks the four-card royal, so hold a straight flush even if it runs 9 through King.

The strategy for 10-7 Double Bonus Poker is as follows:

1. Royal flush – hold.
2. Four of a kind – hold.
3. Straight flush – hold.
4. Four-card royal flush – draw one card.
5. Three Aces – draw two cards.
6. Full house – hold.
7. Flush – hold.
8. Three of a kind – draw two cards.
9. Straight – hold.
10. Four-card straight flush – draw one card.
11. Two pair – draw one card.
12. Pair of Aces – draw three cards.
13. Queen, Jack and 10 of same suit – draw two cards.
14. Four-card flush – draw one card.
15. King, Queen and Jack of same suit – draw two cards.
16. Pair of Kings, Queens or Jacks – draw three cards.
17. Three-card royal flush, other than Q-J-10 or K-Q-J – draw two cards.
18. Four-card open end straight – draw one card.
19. Pair of 2s, 3s or 4s – draw three cards.
20. Jack, 10 and 9 of same suit – draw two cards.
21. Queen, Jack and 9 of same suit – draw two cards.
22. Pair of 5s through 10s – draw three cards.
23. Ace-King-Queen-Jack of mixed suits – draw one card.

24. Three-card straight flush with no high cards, no gaps – draw two cards.

25. Three-card straight flush with one high card, one gap – draw two cards.

26. A-K-Q-10, A-K-J-10, A-Q-J-10, K-Q-J-9, mixed suits – draw one card.

27. Three-card straight flush, one high card, two gaps – draw two cards.

28. Two-card royal flush, no 10 – draw three cards.

29. K-Q-J of different suits – draw two cards.

30. Three-card straight flush, no high cards, two gaps – draw two cards.

31. Four-card inside straight – draw one card.

32. Queen, Jack, 10 of mixed suits – draw two cards.

33. Jack-10 of same suit – draw three cards.

34. Queen-10 of same suit – draw three cards.

35. K-Q, K-J or Q-J of mixed suits – draw three cards.

36. Ace – draw four cards.

37. King-10 of same suit – draw three cards.

38. Three-card flush – draw two cards.

39. One King, Queen or Jack – draw four cards.

Any other hand, discard all five cards.

AUTHOR'S NOTE: Double Bonus Poker is a tricky game, and some readers found confusing one particular strategy variation from regular Jacks or Better. I received enough feedback that I ran the following note in the next column, on May 12, 1995:

NOTE TO READERS: A couple of callers have expressed confusion over last week's strategy chart for Double Bonus Poker, wondering why three Aces is listed at No. 5, separate from other three-of-a-kind hands at No. 8. The big 160-for-1 payoff on four Aces is the difference. Many video poker hands fit more than one category, and as with previous video poker strategy charts, the correct play for such a hand is the one highest on the list.

For example, a full house with three Aces and two Queens would fit No. 5 (three Aces), No. 6 (full house) and No. 16 (pair of Kings, Queens or Jacks). In this case, you would play the hand as three Aces, breaking up the full house, because of the four-Ace bonus. The bonus on other four-of-a-kinds is not large enough to merit breaking up a full house; therefore, three-of-a-kinds other than Aces are listed lower on the chart.

❧ 59 ❧

Can Betting System Up Odds for Winning?

A shuffle through the Gaming mailbag:

DEAR JOHN: *I like to play roulette and watch the numbers board to try to figure out a pattern—for example, whether out of the last 20 numbers 13 are odd and the other seven are even, or whether the board shows more red numbers than black. Is there a higher percentage of winning per gaming session if I bet 18 numbers on the inside—all odds—while still betting on odd every spin and split-covering 0 and 00?*

– Ted Ross, Bridgeview

Answer: The house percentage is 5.26 percent on each bet you describe, and if you play them in combination, the house edge is still 5.26 percent. To take the combination first, let's say you play one chip on the inside on each of the 18 odd numbers in single-number bets, paying 35-1. You also play 18 chips on the outside bet on odd, an even-money wager. Then you split two chips across 0 and 00 at 17-1, so you are betting a total of 38 chips on each spin. In a perfect sequence of 38 spins in which each number—1 through 36 plus 0 and 00—comes up once, you will bet 1,444 chips.

Each of the single-number bets will win once, bringing a return of 648 chips (18 winning wagers at 35-1 bring 630 chips in winnings, plus the player keeps the 18 chips wagered that did not lose); the bets on odd will win 18 times, also returning 648 chips (324 in winnings, 324 in chips retained), and the split bet on 0 and 00 will win twice, giving you

72 more chips (68 in winnings, four retained). That leaves you with a total of 1,368 chips, meaning you've lost 76 chips, or 5.26 percent, in the sequence.

Now let's say you play the same 38 chips per spin, all on the outside bet on odd. Each winning wager will return 76 chips—38 in winnings plus 38 in wagers retained. In the same perfect sequence, you will win 18 times, returning 1,368 chips—the same as in the combination example.

You're unlikely ever to really see this perfect sequence of spins—sometimes your odd numbers will come up more frequently than 18 times per 38 trials, sometimes they'll come up less. But over the long haul, the percentages will hold up, and making several different bets at a time can't change that.

DEAR JOHN: *Can't the Gaming Board do something about the tactics of the riverboat casinos on their pushing blackjack bets to a higher minimum? We recently went to the Grand Victoria in Elgin. We went midweek and made the first boarding at 8:30 a.m. There was a rush of players for the four $5 tables. The casino left the minimum at $5 until 11 a.m. when the next cruise entered. They then pushed two of the $5 tables to $10 and opened another table at $5 to catch the new players. About one-half hour later they pushed that table to $10, leaving just two of the 26 tables at the $5 minimum.*

– Warren Wieland, Prospect Heights

Answer: It is left to the discretion of the casinos to set table minimums. All the riverboats in the Chicago area raise table minimums on more crowded cruises. From the casinos' perspective, it's just economic common sense—why keep table minimums low when the boat is full of customers willing to risk more money? The problem for those who like to play in Elgin is that Grand Victoria is crowded nearly all the time, and there has been more demand for space at the tables than even the casino operators dreamed before the boat opened. The space crunch results in higher table minimums earlier in the day than at other operations in the area. It doesn't look as if that's going to change soon.

Personally, I prefer the Las Vegas approach to changing table minimums. I've frequently been at tables in Vegas when a supervisor approached, changed the sign and announced that the table minimum was being raised for new players. Anyone already sitting at the table would be allowed to play at the old minimum. But with fewer gaming positions, some riverboats seem to be in more of a hurry to get the table full of higher-betting players.

❧ 60 ❧
Bettors Need Not Worry
Whether Shill Is Gone

A shuffle through the Gaming mailbag:

DEAR JOHN: *Do the riverboat casinos in Illinois use shills? At the black-jack tables, I see players making plays so bad that I have to think the house is trying to mess up the game for the other players. I saw somebody hit on 17 the other day. He had to be working for the casino.*

– Name withheld

Answer: It's a lot more likely that the players you've observed are simply bad players, rather than shills or house players. For one thing, bad players don't really change the odds of the game. We tend to remember when a bad play costs us a hand, but conveniently forget when a bad play helps us. Those situations balance out in the long run. It gives the house no extra advantage to place a bad player at the table.

Also, space is still at a premium on local riverboats. A spot being taken by a shill is a spot not available to a player who will risk his own money.

Finally, the Illinois Gaming Board must license all casino employees, with a specific job listing. There is no employment category for house players or shills, and the board would not look favorably on their use.

House players at table games are most commonly used at casinos that have a lot of space and empty tables. Some customers are uncomfortable being the first player to sit down at a table, so house players are used to break the ice. Some casinos also use slot machine shills—check out some of the smaller places in downtown Las Vegas sometime. These casino employees sit at specially souped-up machines that pay at a very high rate so that customers see winning combinations being hit and hear coins clinking into the tray. The house hopes that will encourage customers to play other machines with a normal house advantage.

DEAR JOHN: *I would like to know the odds of receiving a royal flush in Caribbean Stud poker. This has been puzzling us for some time.*

– Todd and Little Ray, no address

Answer: Caribbean Stud is a variation of five-card stud poker. In any five-card stud game, the royal flush should show up about once in every 640,000 hands.

The recent world-record $390,000 Caribbean Stud jackpot paid at Harrah's Joliet and the jackpot that stood at more than $460,000 at Joliet's Empress last week bring up an interesting point. After a jackpot is hit and the progressive meter is reset (at $10,000 at some casinos, $5,000 at others), the $1 side bet on the progressive jackpot is extremely negative for the player. However, when payouts for flushes, full houses, four of a kinds and straight flushes are factored in along with the big payoff for a royal flush, the bet is said to "go positive" as the meter nears $300,000. Then the bet carries a positive expectation—if you played only with the meter at that level or higher, in an infinite number of hands, you would be expected to win more money than you lose.

In the short term—and these big jackpots exist only in the short term—most players will lose all their bets on the progressive meter. One customer will be a big winner when the royal flush shows up, and others will show smaller wins on hands from a flush on up.

DEAR JOHN: *What is the best strategy for playing slot machines? Do you put in only a few coins and then move to another machine? Do you put your whole budget in one machine? Just how should one play it? Also, how are the machines programmed? Are they set to pay off once every 24 hours, for example? Is it a random hit-and-miss situation, where if in the right place at the right time you get lucky?*

– John L. Doering, Morton Grove

Answer: Slot combinations are random, or as close to random as humans can program the random number generator that determines the combinations to be. So in the long run, it makes little difference if you stay at the same machine or move around. Personally, I prefer to move around if I have several pulls in a row with no hits, but stay put if the machine's giving something back. But that's just for my own mental state—there's no way of knowing when a machine is going to hit.

More important than whether you stay put or move is to limit your losses and lock up part of your winnings. If you sit down with a 100-coin stake, think about taking a break when it drops to, say, 80 coins. And if you hit a 100-coin jackpot, put some aside, not to be replayed regardless of how the rest of the day goes. That way, you'll be certain of walking out of the casino with something, and will have a shot at occasional winning sessions even if a big jackpot doesn't come.

☙ 61 ❧

Iowa Casinos Gain Edge
With Liberalized Rules

For most Illinois riverboat casinos, business is booming. Last month, for the first time since gaming opened in the state in 1991, casinos totaled more than $100 million in adjusted gross receipts.

But the boom has passed by Casino Rock Island in Rock Island and the Silver Eagle near Galena. Alone among Illinois casinos, they are in a period of declining revenue. The reason isn't difficult to pinpoint: Dockside gambling in Iowa has drawn too many customers across the Mississippi River.

The casinos have sought relief in the state Legislature without success. A dockside gambling measure sponsored by Rep. Ron Stephens (R-Troy) was shot down in May. By the time lawmakers can take up the issue again, it may be too late.

Casino Rock Island is making no direct threats to leave Illinois, just as two riverboats left Iowa before that state's gaming laws were changed to eliminate a competitive disadvantage. But Casino Rock Island's share of the Quad Cities market fell from 51 percent to 25 percent when its only competition on the Iowa side of the river was the President in Davenport. And the decline got steeper as a third Quad Cities boat, the Lady Luck in Bettendorf, Iowa, enjoyed its first full month of operation in May.

Casino Rock Island sales and marketing director Bill Renk wonders how long the fight can go on.

"You can tweak what you do with the games and the slots," Renk says, "but are you going to compete with dockside by saying you have loose slots? We've positioned ourselves as having the loosest slots in the Quad

Cities. It can't hurt, right? But how much it helps remains to be seen. People say, 'Yeah, they have loose slots, but you can't get on.'"

In Iowa, which changed its gaming regulations a year ago, customers can get on and off the boats almost at will. Iowa boats must sail a total of only 100 times between April 1 and Oct. 31. Most schedule one early morning cruise, Monday through Friday, and remain dockside the rest of the time. Customers are neither stuck on the water if the losses come too quickly nor forced to leave too soon if a hot streak hits near the end of a cruise.

Most important is that going to a dockside casino can be a spur-of-the-moment decision. In Illinois, customers must wait for one of the scheduled 30-minute boarding periods.

The results have been devastating. Where Casino Rock Island used to gross $3 million to $4 million a month, in April that was down to $1.9 million, compared with $8.5 million for the President. And in May, Rock Island fell again, to $1.4 million.

The news isn't much better in East Dubuque, where the Silver Eagle used to draw 90,000 or more customers and gross close to $3 million each month. In April, admissions were 63,083 and receipts $1.8 million, compared with 75,362 admissions and $2.8 million in receipts for the Diamond Jo, the competition in Dubuque. In May, Silver Eagle held steady, with 62,367 admissions and gross receipts of $1.8 million.

Silver Eagle marketer Ron Vaughn remains hopeful. "I think we can survive," he says. "We'll sure give it our best shot. We'll do all the necessary things, promotional offers, that we can within the guidelines of the Illinois Gaming Board."

But at best, business is a struggle under current conditions.

"This means jobs, revenue for the state and for the cities," Renk says. "I would hope the Legislature would look at that. What are we saying to Illinois businessmen when we let this business go to Iowa?

"All we're asking is that there be fair competition."

AUTHOR'S NOTE: Since this column appeared on June 23, 1995, there has been no relief for the Illinois casinos in direct competition with Iowa riverboats. Casino Rock Island continues to operate, thanks in part to the city of Rock Island kicking its share of the state gaming tax to the casino. Silver Eagle monthly revenues eventually dipped below $1 million. It closed its doors in early December, opting to wait out the winter and reopen later with few table games, mostly just slots and video gaming devices.

❧ 62 ❧
Computers Help Players
Learn Winning Strategies

All casino games are based in mathematics. Perhaps that's why it seems games of chance and the computer were meant for each other.

Even though most games played in the casino predate the personal computer age by decades, even centuries, practice on the computer has become one of the easiest, most effective ways to learn casino strategies. The games that translate best to the computer are the ones that involve the largest elements of skill: blackjack and video poker. But there also is value in playing an easier game, such as Caribbean Stud Poker, on the screen just to establish a comfort level with the rules and conditions of the game before playing it in the casino

Most of the casino programs you'll find in mainstream software stores are multiple-game packs that are fun to play but provide little in the way of instruction or strategy hints. They're colorful and entertaining, but have little more educational value than the hand-held games that seem to be available in any department, drug or toy store these days.

From time to time, I'll be reviewing software that can be used as a learning tool, though most also can be played as games.

Most of the best educational casino software is available only for IBM PCs and compatibles. If any readers know of good, solid learning programs for the Mac, write to me about them and I'll use responses in a future letters column.

Video poker is a product of the computer age, and as a video game with strong elements of skill, it's the casino game that translates best to the home computer. So let's start our software tour with programs featuring two of gaming's heavy hitters—one program by Stanford Wong, the other featuring strategies by Lenny Frome.

Stanford Wong Video Poker, Villa Crespo Software, 1725 McGovern St., Highland Park, Ill. 60035; (708) 433-0500.

Masque Video Poker for Windows, Masque Publishing, Box 5223, Englewood, Colo. 80155; (303) 290-9853.

These two programs share so many of the same strengths that they beg to be discussed together. Both can be played either as games or strictly for practice; both can be set for Jacks or Better, Deuces Wild and Joker's Wild variations; both can be set to warn when the player is making a mistake; both can be set to display the proper strategy before the hand is played out; both can run off millions of simulated hands and display a payback percentage for the simulation.

Those who live in a Windows environment will like the easy familiarity of Masque Video Poker, which requires Windows 3.0 or higher. But the Wong program, written for MS-DOS 3.0 or higher, is plenty easy to use.

An edge for Masque, which also comes in a non-Windows version for DOS 2.1 or higher, is that it includes a booklet on how to play video poker, complete with strategy tables by video poker expert Frome—a real plus for players who do not already have a good video poker strategy book. Strategy tables also can be pulled down on the screen from the Windows menu. The Wong program has no such tables, though it will display estimated values for any way a player chooses to play a hand.

The Masque select mode is also easier to use than the Wong version. In either program, the player may select five cards and see the estimated value for any way to play the hand. Masque offers a 52-card display, and the player need only to point and click to select a card. On the Wong program, the player first must click to select a suit, then click, once for each increase in card denomination—a click to change from 2 to 3, another click to 4, and so on.

But for a more experienced player who already has a basic idea of video poker strategy, the Wong program has one big advantage: Players may change the pay tables from the basic game. If you play frequently on

7-5 Jacks or Better machines, for example, you can change the basic payouts of 9-for-1 on full house and 6-for-1 on a flush to 7-for-1 and 5-for-1, and on each hand you play, Wong's program can display the proper estimated value for the new pay table. Masque does not have that flexibility.

For those who like to play in video poker tournaments, Wong has a more realistic tournament setting that allows players to put limits on both time and number of hands played. There is no timer on Masque tournament play.

Overall, newer players will find it easier to learn video poker strategy concepts on the Masque program; players with more expertise who are looking for an extra edge on varied pay tables will like Wong. Both are outstanding learning tools.

❧ 63 ❧

Americans Visit Casinos
125 Million Times in '94

What's America's national pastime? Between the growth in casino gaming and baseball's post-strike woes, the pass line and Diamond Deluxe slots appear to be attracting more interest than the baseline or the baseball diamond.

Two major surveys released this year have found Americans' habits and attitudes toward gambling reflecting the continuing casino building boom. In the 1995 United States Survey of Gaming and Gambling conducted by the Gaming Research Group, part of the social science research center at Mississippi State University, more than 61 percent of the sampling of 1,500 American adults said they had gambled in some form last year.

The other report, the annual survey of casino entertainment by Harrah's, found theme parks as the only form of entertainment to outdraw casinos last year. Americans visited theme parks 146 million times in 1994, compared with 125 million casino visits. Both far outdistance NFL and NCAA football combined (47 million), arena concerts (30 million), symphony concerts (25 million) or Broadway and touring shows (25 million).

And baseball? Well, Harrah's reported in last year's survey that casinos had outdrawn major league baseball for the first time in 1993. In 1994, the ratio was 2½-1, as baseball drew 50 million fans in its shortened season.

"We knew that gambling has become a growth industry," says Arthur G. Cosby of the Gaming Research Group, which includes researchers from the University of Mississippi and the University of Nevada at Las Vegas, as well as Mississippi State. "Most states have approved either lottery or casino gambling to raise tax revenue or to encourage economic development.

Our survey documents just how dramatic that growth is."

The dramatic growth has been in the newer gaming markets. Harrah's found that while in 1990 41 million of the 46 million casino visits were in the traditional gaming markets of Nevada and New Jersey, by 1993 35 million of the total 92 million visits were in the new markets, and last year 59 million of the 125 million visits were to newer gaming destinations. Fifty percent of the growth in casino visits last year came in the South, with 33 percent in the North Central region, 9 percent in the Northeast and 8 percent in the West. And for the first time last year, the largest percentage of casino visits came from the North Central region—28 percent, compared with 25 percent from the South, 24 percent from the West and 23 percent from the Mideast.

The states generating the most casinos visits, according to Harrah's, were California (14 million), New York (9 million), Illinois, Mississippi, Wisconsin, Pennsylvania, New Jersey and Minnesota (all 7 million to 8 million). Six metropolitan areas generated at least 3 million visits each— New York, Philadelphia, Los Angeles, Minneapolis-St. Paul, Memphis and Chicago.

Harrah's found that casino visits were made by people from 30 percent of U.S. households last year, up from 27 percent in 1993.

The Gaming Research Group includes lotteries, bingo halls, horse racing, dog racing as well as casino gaming in concluding that 61 percent of U.S. adults gambled last year. By its count, 54 percent of Americans bet at least once in state-run lotteries last year, 24 percent wagered in casinos, 8 percent at horse and dog tracks and 7 percent at bingo halls.

Particularly meaningful for the future expansion of gaming could be the section on acceptance of casino entertainment in the Harrah's study. Only 8 percent of those surveyed said casino entertainment is "unacceptable for everyone." Fifty-nine percent called casino entertainment "acceptable for anyone," while 33 percent called it "acceptable for others, but not for me."

The Gaming Research group reports that a majority of adults in all age groups except those over 70 reported gambling in the last year, more men gambled than women, more whites than non-whites, and those at the lowest education levels gambled less than those with more education.

That parallels the Harrah's study, which found that 52 percent of casino players have at least some college education, that the median household income of casino players is $41,000 a year, compared with $30,400 for the U.S. population as a whole, and that the median age of casino players is

46. Harrah's reports that 56 percent of casino players are women.

So where does the casino industry go from here? More and more, bigger and bigger, Harrah's predicts. More riverboats, more tribal casinos, and, with Louisiana having become the first state since New Jersey in 1978 to approve a full-scale land-based casino, more gaming on land.

Added to the expansion of riverboat gaming in Missouri and the possibility of Indiana riverboats coming on line later this year, that could mean 1995 will be the first year in which the majority of casino visits are made outside Nevada and New Jersey.

❧ 64 ❧

Reader Drawn to Story
Of Magnet on the Slots

A shuffle through the Gaming mailbag:

DEAR JOHN: *I recently heard of an incident in Mississippi where a woman hit for $11,000 on a dollar slot machine. Before they paid her, they asked if she had any magnets on her, did she have any lucky trinkets with magnets; they searched her purse and they frisked her. Also they told her it would be best that she left and they escorted her to the city limits. I would like to know why she received this type of treatment.*

– J. Carter, Gary

Answer: The casino company you mentioned in your letter says it has no record of any such incident. And an $11,000 jackpot is large enough in that market that it would be memorable regardless of the outcome. The company, which is regarded as reputable within the industry, says either it would give a publicity rush to the big winner, or it would trumpet the news that it caught a slot cheat.

On older machines, cheats sometimes used magnets to disable the timing mechanism and let the reels float until they could line up a winning combination. But today's slot machines are not so vulnerable to magnets. Casinos do not routinely check for magnets when a big jackpot is hit, but they may check the combination showing on the reels against the computer record of the pull. If they do not match, an investigation follows.

DEAR JOHN: *You made a comment that in Las Vegas certain slot machines are souped up with a shill playing it. I thought that by state laws all slots are set paying out the same. Explain please.*

P.S. Can you play a souped-up machine after the shill leaves?

— Joseph L. Venckus, La Grange Park

Answer: Machines are not required to pay out the same percentage, not in Nevada or any other state. Most states have a legal minimum payout, and some also have a legal maximum, but machines with widely different paybacks can be placed side-by-side in the same casino.

At some of the smaller Nevada casinos, shills play machines paying in excess of 100 percent, and return all winnings to the house. When a shill leaves he's either replaced by another shill or the machine is shut down. I once saw a man playing two adjacent $1 machines, hitting winning combinations on every pull. As one machine was paying out, he played the other. He was surrounded by dozens of racks of $1 tokens. The machines were roped off, and security guards stood at either end of the rope. Were those machines opened to all comers when this player left? Of course not.

DEAR JOHN: *Some questions about Caribbean Stud Poker. What is the house percentage advantage? Does the dealer's exposed card affect the way you play your hand? When do you bet on anything less than a pair? Would you bet an Ace-King hand? Is there an advantage at playing at a full table or a less full table? What are the odds of being dealt a royal flush, straight flush, flush, full house and four of a kind?*

— John B., Chicago

Answer: The house has about a 5.6 percent edge in Caribbean Stud. Your questions on the dealer's exposed card, playing less than a pair and playing Ace-King tie in together. Play all pairs, but play Ace-King only when one of the cards in your hand matches the dealer's exposed card. Do not play hands of less than Ace-King. The number of players at a table makes no difference. And the true odds are 650,000-1 against a royal flush, 70,000-1 against a straight flush, 4,000-1 against four of a kind, 700-1 against a full house and 500-1 against a flush.

DEAR JOHN: *I am a longtime player of slot machines, and something always puzzled me. I see people putting one coin in a three-coin machine and they play that way for a long time. What I would like to know is does that one coin get the machine through its cycle or is it based on the amount of money the machine takes in before it gets in a paying cycle?*

— Joan Konkel, Rockey Mount, Mo.

Answer: Neither the number of coins played nor the amount of pulls in the handle make any difference to the random number generator that determines the combinations that come up on the reels. The RNG constantly, and at a very high speed, generates numbers corresponding to reel combinations, even when the machine is not in use. Which combinations you hit are an accident of timing. If you played a split second faster, or slower, you'd see different combinations on the reels—not necessarily winning combinations, but different ones.

❧ 65 ❧
Small Edges Can Give
Player Bigger Bankroll

There are many large issues every player should consider before going to a casino: what size bankroll to bring, how best to manage money, what games to play and the best bets and strategies in those games.

But there also are some little tips to file away in the back of your mind. Some rarely, if ever, come into play; others may happen several times each visit to a casino, but make a difference of only a few cents at a time. Still, when there's a decision to be made that can mean a little extra edge, no matter how minute, there's no reason to give that edge to the house.

Remember these small edges next time you head for the casino:

Hold the fifth card: Deuces Wild video poker is popular largely because of the big secondary jackpot for four deuces. Not only is a royal flush with the full five coins played worth the same 4,000-coin payback available in Jacks or Better, but four deuces in the most common versions are worth 1,000 coins. There also are machines with four-deuce paybacks of 2,000 coins, 2,500 coins and even 3,000 coins.

That's a jackpot worth protecting. So what happens when you're dealt four deuces in the first five cards? That fifth card means nothing—it makes no difference on the payout if the extra card is a 3 or an Ace or anything in between.

Still, the best play is to hold all five cards. Why? On the glass of many electronic gaming devices, whether reel slots, video poker, video blackjack or video keno, you'll find the words "Malfunction voids all play," or words to that effect. What if the machine malfunctions, and in a one-in-a-zillion glitch, the discarded fifth card is replaced by a fifth deuce? Since the machine is supposed to be dealing from a 52-card deck containing only four deuces, any casino employee who glances at the screen would know there was a malfunction. The casino could void the play and refuse to pay the jackpot.

You'll probably never see this happen, but why take chances? Hold the extra card.

Play the pink chips: At most blackjack tables in Las Vegas, the tray holding chips is equipped with plenty of $1 tokens and quarters for the purpose of making change. If a player with a $5 bet hits a blackjack, the 3-2 payoff means he wins $7.50, which is paid with one $5 chip, two $1 tokens and two quarters. You cannot play the quarters at the table.

In other parts of the country, many casinos use pink $2.50 chips instead. A blackjack on a $5 bet brings one $5 chip and one $2.50 chip. These you can play. Many players wait until they have two pink chips and use those to make a $5 bet, or simply toss 'em to the dealer as a tip.

But what happens if you stack four $1 chips on top of a $2.50 chip and make a $6.50 bet instead? Now if you hit a blackjack, the 3-2 payoff means the house owes you $9.75. Some casinos that use pink chips also keep quarters at the table just for this situation, but others have no denomination lower than $1. They can't make change, so most round to the nearest dollar. In this case, instead of $9.75, you'll get $10.

Ask at the table what the house rules are if you hit a blackjack with a pink chip in play. If you find a generous house that always rounds up, then play the pink chip, even with an odd number of dollars as the rest of your bet. For example, a $7.50 bet will bring you $11.25 on a blackjack if the house can make change. If not, a house that rounds to the nearest dollar will give you $11, and a house that always rounds up will give you $12. In a casino that rounds to the nearest dollar, play the pink chip only when the remainder of your bet is an even number—bets of $4, $6, $8 and so on will bring a little bonus with your blackjack.

Play an even number of coins: The problem with most video blackjack machines is that blackjacks pay only even money instead of 3-2. So those few machines that pay 3-2 on blackjacks are treasured by players.

But remember that the machine can't return less than a full coin. On a quarter machine, a blackjack with one coin played would mean a 3-2 payoff, which should bring 37.5 cents. The machine is not equipped with 12.5-cent tokens, so you'll get only a quarter back.

To take advantage of the rule, you'll need to play an even number of coins. A blackjack with two coins played will bring a three-coin payout; if four are bet, you'll get six back, and so on. However, the machine can't pay 4.5 coins on a three-coin bet, or 7.5 coins for five.

Play an even number of coins. Don't give that edge to the house.

⹩ 66 ⹠

Playing to Win
In Three Tournaments

LAS VEGAS—Three blue sevens three times in 10 minutes—it was the stuff of dreams for any slot-machine player.

And 12 hours later, I hit those blue sevens—the top jackpot on the Magnificent 7s machines—four times in another 10-minute span.

Even on the Sands' souped-up tournament versions of the one-armed bandits, it was a thrill just to see the combinations hit, although it took every one of those jackpots to realize any return on my $10 investment.

That's gambling, Las Vegas tournament-style. Casinos stage tournaments in every game from blackjack to video poker, craps to keno, in hopes that entrants will stick around to drop a few dollars outside the competition.

For players, the opponent becomes other players rather than the house. In some tournaments, all entry fees are returned as prize money. That makes those competitions even-money propositions, the best odds a non-card counter will regularly find in any gambling hall.

Entry fees in big tournaments can be as spectacular as the prizes in others. Caesars Palace held a $10,000 slot tournament last October, the same entry fee it takes to get into the no-limit hold-'em event in the Horseshoe's annual World Series of Poker. Entry often includes free or discounted rooms, tournament shirts and meals. Top prizes can run into hundreds of thousands of dollars, sometimes even exceeding $1 million.

On a recent Vegas trip, I chose three tournaments for players of more modest means—a $199 video-poker tournament at the Tropicana, the Sands' daily $10 slot tournament, and a free blackjack tournament at the Riviera.

My tour started at the Trop for two 20-minute tournament rounds. Each player started with 1,000 credits to be played five at a time—200 hands of video poker in 20 minutes. Prizes, from $10,000 to the winner to $100 for 120th of 240 players, would be awarded at a complimentary brunch the next morning.

It would take two hot rounds with returns exceeding the beginning credits to be in the running for the top prize. Ten minutes into my morning session, I knew I'd have to set my sights lower. I'd played 700 credits before I hit anything better than two pair, with its two-for-one return. I finished with an icy 760 points.

But during afternoon play, four full houses and several flushes helped bring my round to 1,105 points for a tournament total of 1,865—just enough to leave me sweating it out until morning as to whether I'd finish in the money.

Royal flushes are always a hot topic among video-poker players—royals they've hit, royals they've missed, royals they've seen other players hit. At the awards brunch, players were abuzz about one that had been hit the previous evening.

"Did you hear someone hit the diamond royal?" said Jim from California, referring to a special progressive jackpot worth more than $3,800 instead of the usual $1,000 for a royal on a quarter machine. "And she only had four quarters in."

By not playing the maximum fifth quarter, the woman had walked away with $250 instead of $3,800.

Everyone at the table groaned.

After a brunch featuring a carvery with turkey and roast beef, crab cakes, fresh fruit, salads and traditional breakfast fare such as scrambled eggs, bacon and sausage, prizes were announced.

It took 2,400 points to win the tournament, making my total look pretty anemic. But the cutoff for 120th was 1,825, putting me in the money with 40 points to spare. I picked up a $100 bill for 95th place, and was off to the Sands.

The Never-Ending Slot Tournament has been a standard Sands promotion for years, drawing hundreds of players each day. Until recently, the daily first prize was an orgy to sate the appetite of the most fanatical player—the choice of a $500 guarantee or one pull on each of the casino's more than 500 slot machines. Now the top prize is a flat $1,000.

For $10, each player gets the chance to tap away at the button that spins the reels for 10 minutes, and to watch the points add up. The only skill involved is spinning those reels as often as possible in the allotted time. The top 12 in the daylong competition come back at 11 p.m. to play another 10 minutes, with prizes ranging down to three free tournament entries.

About eight minutes into my qualifying round, I had more than 6,000 points, and drew the attention of an attendant.

"Looks good," she said. "Let's see those blue sevens once more just to be safe."

Continually tapping the button as we spoke, I asked how much it had been taking to make the finals.

"Yesterday 7,100 made it," she said. "Let's see those sevens."

Seconds later, my third set of blue sevens lined up for 1,000 points, followed immediately by three triple bars for 120 more. Finally, time expired with 7,614 points on the meter, making me the leader on the board.

"Finals are at 11," the attendant said. "Come back around 10 to check the board."

With all afternoon and evening to go until the finals, I headed for the Riviera for the free blackjack tournament.

Each player is given an imaginary $500 bankroll, and has 15 hands to build that up. The top 12 totals of the day advance to semifinals, followed by finals for six players. First prize is $100 in "action chips," each good for one play at a table. When a player wins a bet with a $5 action chip, it is replaced with a real chip. Win or lose, the action chip is taken away.

The Riviera also gives $50 in action chips—half the top prize—to any player drawing a six-card hand of 21 or less at any time in the tournament.

My big chance came on the second hand, when I had 17 after five cards. Normally, that's a hand to stand on, but the other players and the dealer urged me to go for the bonus. I drew a deuce, and had my $50 in action chips. After that, it seemed to matter little that I lost the hand and soon had no way to reach the approximately $2,000 needed to reach the semifinals.

Back at the Sands after 10 p.m., the leader board showed me in ninth place, good enough to qualify for the finals.

At 11, the 12 of us took our places, and the tournament assumed a game-show atmosphere as an emcee took up his microphone and urged a small crowd that had gathered around to count down to the beginning of the 10-minute finals.

Shortly into the session, my first set of blue sevens hit, and I relaxed, as grateful for the 20 seconds to rest my wrist while the machine added the total as I was for the 1,000 points. About midway through the round, I hit a second jackpot, and was running neck-and-neck with the elderly man seated next to me.

When the third set of sevens came up, I was ahead of my morning pace, and knew I had a shot at the big prize.

"Once more," I thought, "and I'll take my chances."

With less than 30 seconds left, the sevens came once more. Two pulls later, time expired and I had 8,664 points—1,700 more than the gentleman next door.

And a split second later, I knew. Three other players gathered around, offering congratulations.

My tournament tour had come to an end with a $1,000 victory, by that 1,700-point margin.

AUTHOR'S NOTE: The Sands' Never-Ending Slot Tournament has ended since this article originally appeared as a travel piece in 1994, and the Riviera no longer holds its free blackjack tournament. But it's still easy to find tournaments for any size bankroll both on the Las Vegas Strip and in downtown Las Vegas.

❧ 67 ❧

Savvy Bettors Can Stretch
Gaming Dollar With Coupons

LAS VEGAS—There are high-rollers and there are low-rollers.

And then there are couponomists.

That's the term used by the Las Vegas Advisor newsletter to describe vacationers ready to take advantage of this Nevada gambling mecca's money-saving opportunities, many of which are available in casino coupon books.

On a recent visit to Las Vegas, I decided to take couponomy to its extreme by spending a morning casino-hopping without playing a dime of my own money.

Instead of cash, I used coupons and coupon books, most readily available to anyone willing to page through the free tourist magazines found in many hotel lobbies, or to ask for the books at casino welcome centers.

Most coupon books include food and drink discounts and free or discounted souvenirs. But for this morning, I focused on gambling promotions—free slot tokens and gaming chips, $3-for-$2 or $7-for-$5 lucky bucks, anything that would turn the odds in my favor for a few bets. I did not play the Big Six wheel or keno, which are discounted in most coupon books.

All it cost was a few rolled eyeballs from more serious gamblers and the occasional taunt from a dealer as I played the coupons and left.

"They come in here trying to win $2, and they risk $5 to do it," the dealer at the Sands said to others at the table while nodding toward me. "Can you believe it? Why would they do that?"

The answer, of course, is that I was risking $5 to win $7, not $2. If the casino gave those odds on every hand, it'd go broke in a hurry.

One big coupon financed most of the morning—$20 in free slot tokens from the Four Queens, a downtown casino heavy into free coin promotions. The most valuable coupons come with subscriptions to gambling-oriented magazines such as Las Vegas Advisor and Casino Player. But the Four Queens also kicks back $5 coupons to folks who order an $8.95 prime rib in its coffee shop, and even packs $10 coupons into packages of software for a Las Vegas-oriented computer game.

The tokens could be used in most of the Four Queens' slot and video poker machines. I chose a 9-6 Jacks or Better video poker machines. A full house and a few smaller payoffs later, I cashed in for $18.75 and was off to Vegas World.

Vegas World's coupon promised $50 in casino action—$20 in table play and $30 in slot tokens. There are a couple of problems with this deal. Slot tokens and scrip for table play are given in four parts in a time-release program—the player must return every 45 minutes to claim the next part.

Since Vegas World is too far north of the major Strip resorts and too far south of downtown's Glitter Gulch for a player to walk to the next casino and back in 45 minutes, most players must stay in the casino for close to three hours to complete the program.

I stuck it out, using the 45 minutes after registration to eat breakfast. During the second 45-minute break, I drove to the Stardust for its coupon book. That left just one 45-minute period in the casino before the final distribution. Part of that was spent playing a free keno ticket. There was no payoff.

Upon final distribution, I played the $50. The slot tokens must be used in special machines with paybacks the Las Vegas Advisor estimates at 10 percent. My payback was zero. The $20 in table action is in the form of special one-way chips that may be played only once—if you win, you receive a regular casino chip, but the special chip is taken away. I played blackjack at $2 a hand. I won four hands, including a double-down, and lost five. That gave me $10, bringing my total for the morning to $28.75.

Stardust coupons included $7-for-$5 offers in six games. I won a hand in blackjack and a pass-line bet in craps, lost a bet on black on the roulette wheel and one on player in mini-baccarat, and skipped pai-gow poker and the Big Six wheel. Net profit was $4, for a total of $32.75.

"Winsurance" at the Sahara looked intriguing. For $10, the coupon promised $20 in slot action. The extra $10 was issued in tokens to be played on special machines. I repeated my Vegas World experience and received no payback.

All was not lost, however. At $3-for-$2, I won two blackjack hands and split two pass-line craps bets for a Sahara profit of $7 and an overall total of $39.75.

Nearing lunchtime, I made the Sands my last stop. Three $7-for-$5 coupons were good at craps, blackjack or roulette tables. I won only one of three blackjack hands, giving me a $3 loss, as well as the sneer from the dealer.

Still, I wound up with a risk-free profit of $36.75 for the morning. That included $18 in table games, where I won 10 hands and lost 10.

And it was a successful result limited only by time, with many more casinos offering the opportunity to practice couponomy.

AUTHOR'S NOTE: Las Vegas is such a rapidly changing destinations that many of the specifics in this 1993 travel piece have changed. Vegas World is gone, having made way for the Stratosphere Tower. The Sahara has been sold, and its promotions have changed a bit. And the Sands has closed, to make way for a megaresort. But chances to take advantage of coupon offers abound. A profitable good time awaits the disciplined low roller.